Supporting Children with Behaviour Difficulties

A Guide for Assistants in Schools

GLENYS FOX

David Fulton Publishers

London

David Fulton Publishers Ltd
414 Chiswick High Road, London W4 5TF

www.fultonpublishers.co.uk

First published in Great Britain by David Fulton Publishers 2001

10 9 8 7 6 5 4

British Library Cataloguing in Publication Data
A catalogue record for this book is available from the British Library.

ISBN 1-85346-764-2

Typeset by FiSH Books, London
Printed in Great Britain

Contents

Do you recognise this person? . . .

Eyes in the back of the head

Saintly

Radar ears

Broad shoulders

Big heart

Ready for anything!

Speedy

. . . Then read on!

Purpose

The purpose of this book is to enable assistants to work more effectively with children who are described as having emotional and/or behavioural difficulties. It is a book which can complement training courses. It is also a useful book for newly qualified teachers in learning how to work in partnership with assistants to support children who find it hard to conform to normally expected standards of behaviour in school.

Audience

This book is intended as a resource for:

- assistants who work as general assistants in schools and who are likely to encounter children with emotional or behavioural difficulties in the course of their work;
- assistants who support particular children whose behaviour is difficult to manage;
- special needs coordinators and teachers who work with assistants;
- training course providers and assistants on courses;
- newly qualified teachers.

Overview

There are sections on:

- understanding children's behaviour;
- frameworks for planning how to meet children's emotional and behavioural needs;
- strategies which work;
- particular needs, e.g. Attention Deficit/Hyperactivity Disorder;
- teachers and assistants working together to promote good behaviour.

Acknowledgements

Thank you to all those assistants who have the challenging role of supporting children whose behaviour is difficult to manage. Much inspiration has come from their common sense care and desire to make things better for this particularly vulnerable group. Thank you to Adrian Faupel and Liz Herrick for their inspiration and generosity of spirit.

Thank you to Margaret Miller for typing the manuscript and to Simon Tucker for the illustrations. And last but not least, to my children for keeping my feet on the ground and constantly demonstrating that, when it comes to managing behaviour, I have a lot to learn from them!

Introduction

There are many children in our schools who, for one reason or another, find it hard to settle to work because of behaviour difficulties. These pupils challenge the authority of teachers and assistants, and often the authority of their parents. These children and young people arouse in us all a mixture of feelings: irritation, frustration, anger, helplessness, disappointment and sometimes despair. The vast majority of teachers and assistants want to help children to learn how to behave in schools because so often difficult behaviour makes it hard for the teacher to teach and for the child to learn. There is also a consequence in terms of the rest of the class, and the effect that the disruptive behaviour of one or two children has on hijacking opportunities for learning for other children – and this in turn works against the explicit role schools now have in raising standards for all children.

In 1999 a survey of the management of assistants by the University of Manchester's Centre for Educational Needs (Balshaw *et al.* 1999) defined what makes good practice in the way assistants work. This report indicates that successful practice:

- fosters the participation of pupils in the social and academic processes of a school
- seeks to enable pupils to become more independent learners
- helps to raise standards of achievement for all pupils.

This book includes information about how to foster the social participation of pupils in school life, which means making them feel a useful part of the school community. This in turn will enable more independent learning and will affect standards of achievement for the better.

Most behaviour that causes teachers and assistants to complain is of a 'low level' type which can be easily managed when the correct strategies are used. However 'low level' behaviour can sometimes escalate into challenging confrontations if not managed properly. For some pupils, who have got themselves into a downward spiral of difficult behaviour, exclusion from school is sometimes used as a means of removing them from their classmates and from situations which lead to trouble. Exclusion is usually a last resort, so if strategies for behaviour management can be learned, which prevent the need for exclusion, this can only be a good thing.

Over recent years there has been a rising tide of excluded pupils, both in the primary and the secondary sector, although these figures have fallen slightly in the last two years as a result of government initiatives. Figures available from the Department for Education and Employment show that there were about 10,400 pupils who were permanently excluded from schools in England (1998/1999) of whom 83 per cent were boys (DfEE 1998).

It is vital that these high levels of permanent exclusion are reduced because evidence shows that children excluded from schools are more likely to offend, and many do not return to full-time education, and find it difficult to get jobs later in life. There is also evidence to show that excluded children are 'not naughty but needy' and that a significant number of these young people develop mental health difficulties as they grow older.

So the need to support children and young people in developing good behaviour is very clear. Learning to behave is as important for some children as learning the curriculum because unless children can settle to learn they will not reach their potential in terms of academic ability. When behavioural difficulties become persistent they are recognised as resulting in special educational needs and the child will require additional support in school. Assistants are often deployed to give this 'additional support'.

There is a wide range of behaviour patterns under the umbrella term of 'emotional and behavioural difficulties'. This range covers low level and often short-term difficulties to long-term and complex problems. In recent years, more pupils have been given medical labels such as Attention Deficit/Hyperactivity Disorder (AD/HD) or Asperger's Syndrome. Some children in our schools have mental health problems and these children need careful support too.

Assistants in school are likely to meet the full range of emotional and behavioural difficulties in the course of their work, from the child who challenges authority to the child who is withdrawn and passive.

Many books have been written on the subject of children's behaviour and many theories have been advanced. In practice there are no easy answers but there are some proven strategies which can be learned which certainly do work if used with sensitivity and care.

This book sets out to help assistants in their important role of supporting the child and the teacher in minimising 'bad' behaviour and promoting 'good' behaviour. It is intended to help assistants in understanding why children develop behaviours which are difficult to manage and it provides a framework for planning effective behaviour programmes. It is intended as a practical guide which describes ideas and approaches which have proved successful and which assistants can learn, in order to provide effective and sensitive support to this group of children and young people.

Chapter 1

The role of the assistant in giving behaviour support

Supporting children whose behaviour is difficult to manage is one of the most challenging roles which assistants take on. These children may arouse in us a range of feelings such as hopelessness, annoyance and helplessness. However, these pupils can be very rewarding to work with as, in giving support, you will be helping them to develop coping skills for life. As you will see later in this book, assistants are in a unique position to be a positive influence and the good news is that there are particular skills which you can learn to help you in fulfilling this role effectively.

What are my responsibilities?

In your work as an assistant you will be working as part of the learning support team in the school and you will usually be managed by a teacher with particular responsibilities, who in turn is managed by the head teacher. If you work in a junior, infant or primary school, it is often the Special Needs Coordinator (SENCO) who will guide your daily work, but it might also be the class teacher with whom you work most closely. In bigger schools or in secondary schools, again the SENCO might be your manager but it could also be a head of year or a head of a subject department if you work in one subject or curriculum area. (In some schools the SENCO has been re-named the Learning Support Coordinator or the Inclusion Coordinator.) In giving support you are providing additional help over and above what children get from the teacher alone. Teachers, by the nature of their work, give learning support to all pupils and they have the responsibility, delegated by the head teacher, for delivering the learning programmes to all children, whatever their abilities, aptitudes and learning needs. This also applies to the management of behaviour. Teachers are responsible for managing their classes in such a way that children are able to learn. In order to do this and to be effective they must be effective managers of behaviour.

It is important for you to remember that assistants are not teachers and that there are clear boundaries within which the assistants' responsibilities are set. If you are working with pupils who have emotional or behavioural difficulties, then the teacher who manages your work has the responsibility to ensure that appropriate behaviour and learning programmes are planned, followed and monitored and that you yourself are well-supported in your role. Pupils whose behaviour is difficult to manage over a period of time will usually have an Individual Education Plan (IEP) and/or an Individual Behaviour Plan (IBP) or a Pastoral Support Programme (PSP) if they are at risk of being excluded from school. These plans will provide you with guidance about what is being done to help the pupil and will often detail your role in giving behaviour support. In some situations, you might be involved in drawing up the plans, together with the child or young person and the teacher. Sometimes this will also involve the parents or carers.

In your daily work as an assistant you will be working under the guidance of a class teacher or several teachers if you work in a secondary school, to meet the needs of the pupil. There may be occasions when you have to work on your own with the pupil, or with a small group outside the classroom. When 'out of range' of the teacher, you need to work as a responsible adult in ensuring the well-being of each child. You will also need to be clear about your role in implementing the school behaviour policy.

In particular lessons there will be specific routines to follow and for children whose behaviour is difficult you will need to be particularly vigilant at lesson changes. Breaktimes and lunchtimes can also provide 'stress points' for such children as there is not as much structure as in lesson times.

What might I be asked to do?

It is important that you know what your duties are from the start in relation to different pupils. You need to know whether you are working mainly with one pupil or with small groups or sometimes with the whole class.

One of your most important roles, as identified in the University of Manchester research (Balshaw *et al.* 1999), is to 'foster the participation of pupils in the social and academic processes of a school'. This means helping the pupils to take a real part in school life both through positive friendships and achievement in learning. For this to happen effectively the pupil must feel included in school life, so it is important to give support to enable the pupil to remain as a part of the full class group for as much time as possible. This means that withdrawing the child from the class group should be avoided if possible and should only happen if there is disruption to the child's learning or the learning of others if he or she remains in the class.

It is sometimes necessary to work with the pupil as part of a small group, again this should happen within the classroom if possible but sometimes you may be asked to work with a small group outside the classroom. Chapter 6 on managing groups gives practical advice for effective group work.

More rarely you will be asked to work on a one-to-one basis with a pupil. Particular arrangements discussed in the Chapter 7 on managing individual children will help you, should you need to do this. How you might support children is shown in Table 1.1.

Table 1.1 Supporting children (source: Lorenz 1998)

1. **As members of the whole class:**
   (a) responding to individual requests;
   (b) managing behaviour;
   (c) providing praise and encouragement.

2. **As members of a small group in class:**
   (a) keeping pupils on task;
   (b) explaining task requirements;
   (c) supporting written work.

3. **As individuals in class:**
   (a) acting as a scribe;
   (b) delivering a structured programme;
   (c) emotional or behavioural support.

4. **As members of a small withdrawal group:**
   (a) delivering differentiated or structured curricular materials, e.g. corrective reading;
   (b) discussing problems;
   (c) delivering specific group programmes, e.g. social skills activities.

5. **As individuals on a withdrawal basis:**
   (a) delivering structured learning programmes;
   (b) delivering specific therapy programmes or medical procedures;
   (c) individual counselling.

In secondary schools assistants sometimes work with individual pupils, sometimes they are attached to curriculum areas and sometimes to year groups. In terms of behaviour support, the individual or year group arrangement is better as it aids the building of relationships.

Establishing a good relationship with the pupil

In the role of assistant it is extremely important that you work to develop good relationships with the pupil or pupils you support, especially if their behaviour is difficult to manage. These children are sometimes disliked by their classmates and excluded from social groups. Every child needs to be valued but exclusion works to make children feel worse about themselves rather than better. If you can build a positive relationship with the pupil, and encourage others to do so too, then you will be fostering their participation in the social aspects of school life.

You can build this positive relationship by:

- Showing an interest in the child's interests.
- Greeting them by name each day.
- Noticing when they seem upset or worried.
- Giving encouragement for effort.

- Finding something positive to say about them each day.
- Expecting that their behaviour will improve.
- Trusting them with responsibilities.
- Using humour to engage their cooperation.

KEY POINT

Every child needs to be valued. You need work to develop positive relationships with those children who find it hard to behave or settle to learning.

Here are some examples of what your role might include:

- Settling the child into school by having a quiet chat beforehand.
- Sitting close by so you can spot potential 'banana skins' and prevent difficulties from arising.
- Ensuring the child has all the equipment they need so that they can get on without a fuss.
- Giving positive attention to keep the child 'on track'.
- Reminding the child of the behaviour targets they might be working towards.
- Observing the child's behaviour so you can get an idea of what is causing the problem.
- Recording good or bad behaviours.
- Resolving conflicts between pupils.
- Calming situations which are becoming heated.
- Monitoring or tracking a child through their day.
- Providing a 'listening ear' for pupils who need to talk about their problems.
- 'Catching them being good' and providing encouragement for good behaviour.
- Reporting back to the teacher, especially problems or successes.
- Contributing to planning meetings or reviews about the child.

Sometimes the job can seem a little daunting and you may feel 'thrown in at the deep end' but advice and support are available to help you. If you are unsure about anything ask the teachers you work with who will usually be only too happy to lend support.

The SENCO or Head of Year may be able to give you help in dealing with more difficult pupils and there are also external specialists, e.g. educational psychologists or behaviour support teams who are able to provide guidance and support. You need to know that you are not working on your own but as part of a team and that you do not have the sole responsibility for working with the pupils.

If you are not clear about what to do and how to do it then a clear job description is a good starting point. If you don't have one you might need to ask for one. All schools are required to have behaviour (discipline) policies and you will find it helpful to read the one in your school so you know the framework within which the staff operate. For your day-to-day work you will need to understand the 'ground rules' of working to support both the teacher and the child in the classroom, with particular reference to behaviour problems.

An assistant is someone who helps you stay afloat

Where shall I sit in the classroom?

This will depend on the age of the child and the particular classroom activity. You may need to sit very close to a younger child who needs a 'minder' to help in controlling behaviour but older children are not as keen to be seen as different, so you may need to intervene only when necessary. Again, the class teacher will guide you in this.

Age and individual differences need to be considered sensitively when devising support plans for pupils. I recall a young man, James, who had just started at a mainstream secondary school having transferred from a special school for children with emotional and behavioural difficulties. The head teacher of the secondary school had insisted that James had full-time support from an assistant. When I visited James a few weeks into his new school life I asked him how he was getting on 'Well it's OK here' he said 'but there's a woman who keeps following me around, and I wish she'd go away!'. Clearly he wasn't keen to be seen as different from the other young people at the school and I guess the assistant was not having such a good time of it either. Assistance for pupils does need to be sensitively planned to take into account their age and their own views on being supported.

What if something goes wrong?

There are a number of safety issues which you need to be aware of as part of your role. Every employee of the local authority is covered by a general employment insurance policy held by that authority. By law you are deemed 'a responsible adult' and the duties performed by you are delegated to you by the head teacher. If something does go wrong you should discuss the situation with the teacher who is responsible for your work and possibly with the head teacher.

Accidents/incidents

In the case of any accident it must be recorded in the school's incident/accident book. In the case of injury to a child, your first priority is to see that the child is given first aid and that the class teacher or form tutor is informed.

Assistants report a range of fears about what might go wrong when working with children whose behaviour is volatile. These concerns are addressed in the last chapter of this book.

Disclosures

If, during the course of your work with a child or young person, some disclosure of physical or sexual abuse is made to you, then you have a duty, under the Child Protection Law, to inform the head teacher who will take any action necessary.

The 1989 Children Act states that a child's welfare is paramount and safeguarding it and promoting it is a priority. Schools have clear routines to be followed in the case of injury or abuse and it is your responsibility to ensure that you know what these procedures are. If you are not sure, the teacher who is responsible for your work can direct you to the information you need. In your work as an assistant you may well be the first to notice the signs and symptoms which suggest abuse of some kind and you need to know what to look out for.

Concern about abuse

There are certain danger signs which should alert you to possible abuse. However, not all pupils will show the signs described below and sometimes they can occur as a result of depression or anxiety, so you should always discuss concerns with a teacher before doing anything more.

What should I look out for?

Drug abuse

- a deterioration in academic work
- a deterioration in attendance
- a disregard of the conventions of normal behaviour
- dilated pupils
- lack of concentration
- excitability
- mood swings
- unusual rudeness
- particular tiredness as the drugs wear off
- secretive behaviour

Physical abuse

- bruising or unusual marks on arms or legs
- withdrawal

- change in normal behaviour patterns
- flinching when someone is close

Sexual abuse

- change in normal patterns of behaviour
- a deterioration in academic work
- withdrawal
- self-deprecation (e.g. tearing up work)

- reluctance to change for PE
- masturbation in school (in some cases)

There is also evidence to suggest that young people are consuming more alcohol (British Household Panel Survey 2000) so you might also need to be aware of the effects of hangovers on school behaviour.

Here are some questions assistants often ask:

Who sets the rules for the child?

The school behaviour policy is likely to include school rules which teachers may (or may not!) refer to as part of their work with the class. Rules are very useful especially if used positively, and if children understand them, as they help to provide clear boundaries and maintain order. The class teacher is responsible for setting the rules for the child as part of the whole class. If there are no clear rules, you will need to discuss with the class teacher what you might use as guidelines for your work in giving support to the child

What should I do if I see some misbehaviour?

There are likely to be times when you see incidents which the teacher does not, e.g. a squabble or name-calling. You need to know whether you can intervene and, if you do, how you should handle the situation. You should observe how the teacher works and talk with them about how they would want you to react. This may be more complex in a secondary school as there are a number of different teachers to relate to, sometimes with quite different approaches. However, there should be some ground rules which are consistent across the school.

Can I give rewards for good behaviour?

Part of your job is to provide encouragement and support and as part of this you will be giving plenty of praise to the children and young people you work with. Most teachers are very happy for assistants to do this. You will need to negotiate with the teacher about whether

Following the school's behaviour policy

7

you are able to give stickers, certificates or more tangible rewards to the pupils you work with.

Can I provide sanctions (punishments) for bad behaviour?

You will probably be providing some negative messages (shaking of head, a 'look', etc.) to children to communicate disapproval. However, it is important that you negotiate with the teacher if you can go beyond this, e.g. in moving the child away from the group or recommending a detention. It will usually be the case that you report difficult behaviour to the teacher who will decide on an appropriate course of action.

What sort of person do I need to be to do this work?

When assistants are asked what qualities they need to work with children who have behaviour difficulties these are their responses:

- Thick skin.
- Sense of humour.
- Eyes in the back of the head.
- Broad shoulders.
- Big heart.
- Patience.
- Ability to learn from mistakes.
- Belief that children can change.

Most assistants have these qualities and find the work demanding but very satisfying.

Review of role in giving behaviour support

In which areas are you doing well?

Which areas need development?

For each of these statements, please ring the rating scale, which ranges from (1) need little improvement to (6) needs a great deal of improvement.

I am:

• clear about my role in supporting pupils with behaviour difficulties	1	2	3	4	5	6
• working in partnership with teachers to plan for behaviour management	1	2	3	4	5	6
• clear about what are effective strategies	1	2	3	4	5	6
• clear about how to build good relationships with pupils	1	2	3	4	5	6
• in need of training in this area	1	2	3	4	5	6

It will be helpful to discuss your responses with the teachers you normally work with.

Chapter 2

Understanding children's behaviour

In the course of your work as an assistant you are likely to come across a range of children's behaviour which you might find puzzling, challenging, saddening or maddening! In order to help us to understand what makes children behave well or badly in the school environment we need first to understand something about what causes particular behaviour patterns to develop in the first place. We can start to do this by considering the development of both normal and abnormal behaviour patterns in the young child.

Much has been written and debated about the relative contributions of 'nature' and 'nurture' to child development. By 'nature' we mean that each child is born with a unique genetic makeup and will develop with certain features and characteristics which are determined by the parents – there are some inherited physical characteristics which are fixed and which cannot be changed, for instance eye colour, ear shape and foot size. But are patterns of behaviour determined before birth? It can be argued that some behaviours are predetermined in order to get our basic needs met. For example, the behaviours which young babies must display in order for their basic needs to be met are quite clear to us.

It is helpful, as a starting point to consider what Abraham Maslow, a famous psychologist, has to say about the needs of human beings (Figure 2.1).

What are the starting points?

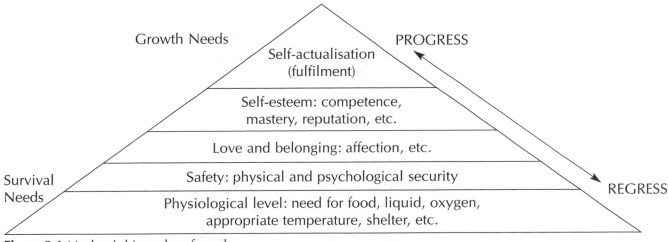

Figure 2.1 Maslow's hierarchy of needs

- This model applies to everybody – not just children.
- We move up and down it according to the situation.
- The higher up the triangle you go the more the needs are under the influence of others, including the teacher or assistant.

This classification of human needs puts the most basic survival needs at the base of the triangle. These are the needs for food, warmth and shelter. If you think of any young baby much of its behaviour is about seeking food and warmth, indeed it will signal hunger, discomfort or cold in ways which cannot be ignored!

A young child has other needs too, the need for love and encouragement. The need to 'belong' to the family or group is also a strong need for human beings and one which guides our behaviour. We will see later in this book how all children seek to belong to the group and that some children have learned the wrong ways of trying to do this!

At the top end of the hierarchy of needs, Maslow describes a need which he calls 'self-actualisation'. This need is about the potential of a human being to feel 'fulfilled' in their life, either through work or through relationships or both – it is about feeling that you have fulfilled the potential you have for doing whatever it is you want to do. The behaviours which drive us to meet this need are more varied than those which drive us to meet more basic needs and are more open to individual choice and influence by external factors and circumstance.

It can be seen then that our behaviours are, in part, designed to help us to get our needs met at a number of different levels. However, we notice a difference in children's temperaments from a very early age. In your work with children in school you will observe that children have different temperaments. Some are shy, some are quiet, some are talkative, some are assertive – there are many personality traits which you will notice. Many parents observe that their own children, who have similar upbringing and environmental influences, are different in personality and temperament.

This leads us to consider that there is a genetic element which affects the way a child might behave and also that often it is similar to another member of the family. You may have heard comments such as 'He is just like his Uncle Jack – he never stopped talking as a child too!'.

What influence does the environment have on behaviour?

Alongside the genetic determinants of behaviour it is clear that the environment, be it family, social or work/school can have a significant influence on human behaviour. Let's look at a number of examples.

Family

Children learn a lot of their behaviour from observing how members of their family relate to one another. They '*model*' their behaviour on those closest to them. Family 'norms' will have an influence on a child's behaviour. If it is usual in the family for meals to be eaten sitting at a table, then the child will learn to do the same. If it is normal for family members to express anger by shouting or swearing at each other the child will learn this behaviour as 'normal'. We all know, from our own experiences that children do as we do rather than what we tell them!

Social

If a young child is in a social situation and another child has a toy which the first child then wants, it is not unusual for the child to reach out and try to take the toy, often causing a conflict. If there were two similar toys, this could be avoided! If an adolescent has friends in a group where it is seen as 'cool' to smoke then that young person will have felt a strong pressure to smoke in order to identify themselves with group 'norms' and feel that they belong to the group. The main influence here is *peer group pressure*.

School

Every school has rules and routines which most children will follow. So if there is a rule of no talking in assembly then this will affect children's natural social inclination to talk and they will learn to keep quiet.

There is usually some negative consequence if they break the rule (such as having to move away from their friends) so they learn that the best outcome for them, i.e. the need to be with the group, will be achieved if they keep quiet and follow the rules and expectations of the group. The main influence in this example is *positive consequences of good behaviour.*

What influence does lifestyle and culture have on children's behaviour?

There is no doubt that children are living in a very different culture from that of 50 years ago. Research shows that they take less exercise and generally eat less healthy food than their grandparents did when they were children.

Today's children are much more exposed to media pressure than their forebears and this undoubtedly has an influence especially in adolescence when the need to belong is at its strongest and so to have the right hairstyle, shoes, clothes and accessories becomes an influence on lifestyle and behaviour. Children are also subject to their parents lifestyle, so with more women now working outside the home, traditional patterns of childcare are changing too. Early experiences of separation from the parents can have a negative effect on children's behaviour, if it is not managed well. Children seem able to develop close relationships with more than just one or two significant adults, if there is love, care and security associated with these relationships and their basic needs are met.

John Bowlby, in his influential book *Child Care and the Growth of Love* tells us that one of the most significant developments in psychiatry over the last century has been 'the steady growth of evidence that the quality of the parental care which a child receives in his earliest years is of vital importance for his future mental health' Bowlby (1953).

There is no doubt that children need a loving carer or carers who can provide a secure home in order to develop feelings of personal security and self-worth. Once this is established then the child is able to make normal social relationships and develop a sensitivity to the needs of others in the community. The chances of being able to fulfil the needs of self-actualisation are much increased for children who have secure and nurturing home backgrounds.

What is 'normal' behaviour development?

Perhaps we should first consider that the word 'normal' has to be interpreted with caution! What is normal behaviour in one circumstance is not normal behaviour in another, e.g. when walking down a busy street you would not normally shout out in a loud voice.

However, should a child you were with step into the road when a car was approaching you might certainly shout out to them. Also, what might be considered 'normal' by one family or culture in terms of social behaviour, might not be considered 'normal' in another. The word 'norm' means an average or standard and is easy to determine when we measure physical characteristics such as height or weight, so we can know for instance what is the average height of ten year olds and what is 'normal' height for that age group and that there is a range of heights which might be 'within the average range'. It is not quite so simple when we look at behaviour as the normal range will be defined by external influences on children, both social and cultural, which affect behaviour.

However, there are certain recognised stages of child development in terms of behaviour which we can expect to see when children are developing within the normal range.

Age 0–2

A new baby, as we have seen, will behave in ways which gain attention for meeting the needs to feed, sleep and be warm and comfortable. In the early weeks of life a baby learns to recognise family members and show pleasure in seeing them, particularly if they are associated with meeting these primary needs! This social behaviour starts at an early stage and develops as the baby starts to explore his or her environment. Playing then follows with new accomplishments being practised with obvious enjoyment. At about nine months many babies take great delight in throwing a toy out of their pram or cot and having the adult replace it for them, thus recognising the social use of another person. Also, most babies at around this age respond with smiles to peek-a-boo games which again require another person to play.

In this early play behaviour it is usually an adult or brother or sister cooperating with a child which delights the child. Babies however seem to have little regard for other babies of the same age and take little notice of one another.

The two year old

A study of over 100 children found that only ten per cent of two year olds actively cooperate in social play with other two year olds (Valentine 1956). Another study of quins, brought up together since birth, found that play was still largely individual at the age of two years (Valentine 1956). Between 2 and 3 years we can observe social behaviour starting to develop. Most children learn to adjust to preschool routines fairly well after a few days. It takes some time to get used to having other children around though and many children play alone most of the time. There are often conflicts and some children may be aggressive to others. This is the age of the 'terrible twos' when the child is wanting to do things for himself or herself and becomes resistant and assertive towards adults. Most parents have had experience of this, and remember only too well the child screaming and kicking in a temper tantrum (usually at the supermarket checkout or some other public place when it is most embarrassing!).

The three year old

By the age of three most children will play cooperatively with another child or in a small group especially if guided by an adult. There can be brief conflicts which are often about the possession of a particular object or toy. It is possible to observe children of this age showing sympathetic or helpful behaviour with other children and with adults. There continues to be occasional conflicts with parents or carers, usually about routines such as dressing, eating or bedtimes, when the child has other ideas about what they want to do!

The four year old

The four year old often prefers to play in small groups and many are bossy and like to show off. Conflicts at this age are fewer and children are learning to share toys.

At this age too, children become more cooperative with adults although some children continue to have upsets and become rebellious, again often when it comes to following adult directions which conflict with what they want to do.

The five year old

By the age of five it is not usual for a child to play regularly alone in school but no more than half of social time is spent playing with others. It is at this age that individual friendships seem to develop and the child becomes less dependent on adults. At home the child is often more settled and amenable.

The primary school years

During these years the child makes great progress in social behaviour. Shortly after starting school, at age four usually, the child learns routines which have to be followed and settles quite quickly into following group behaviour. The child learns the social skills of turn-taking behaviour and the social roles of conforming to normally expected standards of behaviour set by the teacher rather than the parents. If the child has a home experience which is inconsistent in responding to behaviour, he or she will find it more difficult to settle in school.

In the primary school years the child learns that he or she must take account of the actions and feelings of others – not to do so leads to trouble! This is harder for some children than others. By the end of this stage, the child who is developing normally will have friendship groups, be able to take part in team games and will follow school rules and routines and have an understanding of why these controls are necessary. Concepts of 'fairness' and 'unfairness' develop. It is at this stage too, that children learn to adapt behaviours from one environment to another.

The secondary school years

During these years there are significant changes in social awareness and behaviour. The child reaches puberty and, apart from all the physical changes, there are emotional changes and development.

The need for friendship groups seems to become stronger as the young person seeks to 'belong' to the peer group rather than the family. At this stage the influence of other young people is clear, and any parent will be aware of the influence of fashion and music on many teenagers. At this stage it is also normal for the young person to question parental authority as he or she seeks to become less dependent on them.

Sometimes this spills over into school and there maybe 'healthy' conflicts which follow. As sexual awareness develops the young person is much more influenced by the need to develop partnerships and behaviour starts to be influenced by this need. Mood swings are common and it often seems to parents that their previously compliant child has become something of an 'alien', but this is normal and in fact is part of healthy social development as the teenager seeks to develop as an independent person in their own right, and to begin the process of separation from the parents. A recent study, carried out by Essex University in 2000 surveyed the lifestyles of 11–15 year olds (British Household Panel Study 2000). It revealed a rise in alcohol consumption, smoking and contact with drug users as children enter their teens. By the age of 15, nearly 60 per cent of adolescents admit to having friends who use drugs and 70 per cent claimed to have consumed alcohol recently. Also noted was a worrying trend towards vandalism, truancy and distrust of the police. These signs of growing disaffection at the onset of adolescence are borne out by young people's attitude to school. While most pupils continue to like most of their teachers and recognise the importance of doing well at school, these positive attitudes weaken as they get older, most noticeably in boys. The majority of pupils will behave well in school and do not become difficult to manage, but as an assistant you need to understand the influences on children which affect behaviour in school and that adolescence presents a particular set of challenges to both young people, their parents and their teachers.

Children are not angels and all experience some disturbance in behaviour patterns as they grow and indeed challenge to authority can be seen as healthy and normal – there is a streak of mischievous behaviour in many children which can be interpreted possibly as creative, and fun seeking. Some very successful people (a minority it must be said) admit to having been really difficult to manage at school, and found it hard to conform to the demands of authority.

In your work as an assistant you will become aware of a range of 'problem' behaviours in the classroom. These will range from mild 'low level' disruptions to full-blown tantrums or defiance. Assistants who work with children have noted a number of behaviours as those causing concern.

What 'problem' behaviours will I see in the classroom?

It is important to note that most classrooms are well-managed by teachers and most behaviour problems are of the 'low-level' type. It is rare to have major outbursts or fighting in class and if or when it does happen it is the responsibility of the teacher to react appropriately. If you are working with a particularly difficult child then you need to sit down with the teacher and plan just who will do what if a major problem should occur.

What is the child's behaviour trying to communicate?

All behaviour has a reason or a purpose and, as we have seen, we behave in certain ways to fulfil certain needs. However, it is sometimes quite difficult to decide what need the child is trying to meet but we have to consider this if we are going to be effective in our work. It is made all the more difficult sometimes because we take the behaviours at face value and do not look behind what we see in front of our eyes.

OK you blew the first day but tomorrow is the second day of the rest of your life

Perhaps you have had experience of trying to put socks and shoes on a reluctant three year old who is shouting 'I hate you – go away!'. Of course we don't take this at face value but we understand that what the child wants is to carry on playing or sleeping or eating or whatever he or she might have been distracted from.

One of the most basic human needs is the need to communicate. If a child has a learning difficulty which hinders or prevents communication he or she will use increasingly simpler ways of getting their message across (such as, that he or she is happy, tired, unhappy, scared or whatever). Unfortunately, many of the simplest ways of communicating involve behaviour which the rest of us find unacceptable, such as demanding, swearing, tantruming and so on. If the child is using these unacceptable behaviours in order to communicate, then we can reduce or even eliminate the behaviours by teaching the child a better way to communicate the same message that they are currently sending by their inappropriate behaviour. The trick, of course, is to identify what the message is that they are trying to communicate, this is sometimes obvious, but can be subtle. If it is not obvious, the best ways of establishing it is through discussion with teachers and through trying different ways of working with the child.

Things children need to communicate

Self needs:
Immediate gratification *(I want it now)*
Task avoidance *(I don't want to)*
Escape *(I don't want to)*
Panic *(I'm scared)*

Social needs:
Attention seeking *(Look at me)*
Power seeking *(I want to be in charge)*
Escape by avoidance *(Don't expect me to do it . . . I can't)*
Revenge *(I don't want to be part of this group anyway)*

> 'The difficult behaviour is not the problem. It is the solution (for the child). The problem is finding a better solution for the child.'
> (La Vigna 1992)

Skills to teach children who communicate inappropriately

Functionally equivalent skills: What behaviour could we teach the child in order to communicate their needs more effectively?
Functionally related skills: What else does the child need to be able to do in order to use an alternative, better behaviour to communicate the same message?
Coping or tolerance skills: Life is never perfect – how can we teach the child to cope with frustration, criticism, etc?

The following are some behaviours which may need reinterpretation to decide what need the child is trying to meet and what the child is trying to communicate.

The pupil may be described as ...	But this could be ...	The need ..
• Stubborn	• Low self-esteem and fear of failure 'I don't want to'	• To belong and seen as successful by the group
• Aggressive	• Lacking in verbal skills – frustration makes him/her lash out	• Need for social acceptance 'I want to be in control'
• Disruptive	• Unable to cope with work	• Need for attention 'Look at me'
• Unpleasant to others in the class	• Feelings of rejection 'I don't feel part of this group'	• To belong and be included
• Inattentive	• Poor concentration skills 'I can't do it'	• Quiet environment and positive attention
• Attention seeking	• Attention needing	• Positive attention 'Look at me'
• Stealing (e.g. food)	• Survival	• Hunger 'I want it now'

In your work as an assistant you will wear many 'hats'. You will need to put on your 'detective' hat in order to interpret what the child's behaviour means and this will help you to plan your way of working.

Supporting children with emotional and behavioural difficulties

If 'low level' behaviours escalate and become persistent and of concern, then we describe children as having emotional and behavioural difficulties (EBD). This is usually when their behaviour seems to fall out of the 'normal' age appropriate range we would expect to see in a child.

In the course of your work as an assistant you will come across a considerable number of children who need support because of emotional or behavioural difficulties. The 1981 Education Act recognises that emotional and behavioural needs are special educational needs because no child can learn optimally if they are unsettled or unhappy in school for whatever reason (DES 1981).

Sometimes these difficulties are caused as a result of physical, sensory or learning disability but often they are rooted in difficult home backgrounds. There is usually a combination of factors which come together to cause the child to exhibit signs of emotional or behavioural difficulty. In a recent study of pupils considered to be 'at risk' of exclusion from their secondary schools, all had recent or current traumas in their home life, 75 per cent had poor reading skills and 25 per cent were identified as having quite marked signs of mental health problems (bulimia, fire-setting, etc.).

What do we mean by emotional and behavioural difficulties?

Emotional and behavioural difficulties is a blanket term which includes a very wide range of conditions – perhaps the only characteristic these share in common is that the children experiencing them are both troubled and troubling to those who come into contact with them.

The emotional difficulties which lead to interpersonal and social problems range from 'internalising' behaviour, e.g. withdrawal/shyness, depression, extreme anxiety and compulsions, to 'acting out' behaviours (sometimes called conduct disorders) e.g. extreme aggression (to people or property), anti-social behaviour, bullying, defiance. As we have seen, if a child receives inadequate emotional nurturing from the parents or carers, particularly at an early age, then the likelihood of emotional and behavioural difficulties is high. Physical and sexual abuse also increase the likelihood of emotional and behavioural difficulties.

Learning difficulties can also cause emotional problems for children. A sensitive educational environment and curriculum at the right level is necessary.

There are many factors which indicate difficulties of this kind and the vast majority of children, at some point in their school lives, will have some emotional and behavioural problems. Children with special needs of any kind often experience these difficulties as part of their perception of themselves as being 'different'. However, it is when problems persist over a long period of time and become severe and complex, that additional support will be necessary.

Pupils experiencing severe emotional and behavioural difficulties may need special provision where small class groups and a high level of adult attention is offered. There are many pupils in our mainstream schools who also show these difficulties and schools report increasing numbers of such pupils. Assistants play a significant part in supporting them and making it possible for them to remain in their local schools. The majority of these children do not achieve what they are capable of in academic subjects at school because no child can learn effectively if he or she is troubled inside and has feelings of worthlessness.

KEY POINT

Behaviours are learned and can be changed.

Chapter 3

The importance of self-esteem

The dictionary describes self-esteem as 'good opinion of oneself: self-respect – the extent to which we perceive ourselves to be worthwhile and capable human beings'. It is the judgement or view we hold about ourselves based on a whole lot of life experiences, and, although it can vary from time to time, each person has a level of self-esteem which they carry with them wherever they go and it is important because it can have a big influence on how people behave, react and learn. Self-esteem is about liking ourselves. It is linked to the feelings we have about our competence or ability in important parts of our life.

A helpful way of defining what we mean by self-esteem is provided by Denis Lawrence in his book *Improved Reading Through Counselling* (1973), quoted in *You can...You Know You Can: A self-concept approach* (Maines and Robinson 1988):

What is self-esteem?

Self-concept
Self-concept is a global term which includes all aspects about the way we feel about ourselves. It is with us from the very beginning of our lives, affected by all our experiences, acceptance and rejection, success and failure. Under the self-concept umbrella we find three features:

Self-image
Self-image is the picture we hold of ourselves, all our abilities and attributes. It includes ideas about our appearance, intelligence, physical skills and about our place in society, a series of snapshots in a photo-album.

*Self-image is built and modified through our perceptions of the way other people, significant others, behave towards us. These **significant others** are the adults, usually parents and later teachers (and assistants!), by whom we are valued, accepted and affirmed or rejected and criticised. Their attitude to us helps us to form our internal picture of ourselves.*

Our self-image goes with us at all times and influences our behaviour.

Ideal self
Alongside our self-image we carry another picture, an ideal self. This is the slim, witty, intelligent and charming person we would really like to be, and, like self-image, it is formed by our perceptions of the way we are seen by other people. If, from our earliest days, we live with the

---

notion that our parents and significant others would like us to be different, better than we are, then ideal self is likely to be seen as an unattainable goal. We might as well give up.

Self-esteem
Self-esteem is formed when we match up these two pictures, self-image and ideal self. If self-image is good and ideal self is a realistic and attainable goal (with effort and opportunity), then self-esteem is high. We have the confidence to attempt difficult things and if we sometimes fail we can cope.

But if there is a conflict between self-image and ideal self, if self-image is poor and ideal self is way out of reach, then self-esteem is low. What is the point of trying anyway? We don't stand a chance.

How does self-esteem affect behaviour?

Children with high self-esteem tend to be able to discount areas where they are less competent, but children with low self-esteem are unable to do this and tend to be more affected by difficulties. Children with low self-esteem note negative comments that confirm their own view of themselves and do not believe that 'good' comments can relate to them. In other words, they will select out of the environment those things that tend to confirm their beliefs about themselves. Low self-esteem is a key factor in causing behaviour problems and in poor academic achievement. Children need to believe they are valued as members of the school and have some control over their school lives. In your role as an assistant, you are likely to be one of the main adult influences on the pupils you work with.

In fact many assistants play a big part in helping children feel good about themselves. You can have a real influence for the good, especially if you can develop skills which boost the child's self-esteem. As an assistant, if you can help children raise their own self-esteem and feel better about themselves then you will enable them to become better learners and more settled in school.

KEY POINT

You are a powerful influence on the child and can be a real force for positive change in the child's behaviour and attitude – don't give up!

Money in the pocket

Barbara Maines and George Robinson have developed a whole range of excellent materials which help teachers and assistants to support children in developing positive self-esteem (Lucky Duck Publications). They provide a wonderful analogy for understanding what self-concept is. They call this 'money in the pocket':

Many of the situations children face when they come to school may involve them attempting new and difficult tasks. They face the risk of failure each time and that takes some confidence. We use the phrase 'money in the pocket' for two reasons.

Firstly it helps us to realise why some children give up so easily. Like a gambler who needs money to place a bet, money he can afford to lose, a child needs a fund of self-concept before he can put himself at risk. Without the secure knowledge that even if he fails he will still be valued and will succeed again another time, a child is likely to avoid the attempt altogether.

The second reason is that, rather than making us feel helpless because factors outside our control are undermining our pupils' self-concept, it helps us to feel that there is something that we can do. We may not be able to turn a 'poor' child into a 'rich' one in terms of self-concept, but we can keep putting something in his pocket and we can protect him from losing everything if he takes the risk and fails.

Children come to you with different levels of self-concept and those with high self-concept are likely to achieve the best results. We can make the comparison with money; those with the most money in their pockets can take risks, try new things, afford to risk a little and even if they lose some they are not poor.

The child with low self-concept is like a child with very little money. He can't afford to gamble because he runs the risk of failing and being left with nothing at all.

(Maines and Robinson 1988)

To extend this analogy – as an assistant you must do all you can to put money in the child's pocket. You will find that some children seem to have holes in their pockets so the money falls through! But this should not stop you as you will find that the more money you put in, the more chance there is of some staying put.

Keep putting money in his pocket

What affects self-esteem?

Self-concept starts to form in the very early stages of life. Early childhood experiences are crucial in laying the foundations of future positive self-esteem. We have seen in the last chapter just how important it is for children to have parents or carers who are loving and encouraging. The most significant person in the early years is, of course, the parent but when the child starts school his or her life is influenced by more than just parent/carer or close family. These influences come from 'significant others' and these are usually the teachers and assistants who see the child frequently. As the child grows, other members of the class or friends can also become significant others. All these people have the power to influence self-concept.

The attitude of others is really important in determining the level of self-esteem: the more we believe that others value us, the higher will be the regard in which we hold ourselves. For children, up to about 15, significant others are parents, teachers, assistants, peer group and close friends.

The development of self-esteem with age

We are not born with a sense of self-esteem: it develops with age. In the age range 4–7 children form their self-image from the judgements they make about their physical and intellectual competence, social acceptance and behaviour.

During middle childhood, about 8–12, the main areas they judge themselves by are ability at school, athletic competence, physical appearance, acceptance by others of their age and behaviour. In adolescence three further areas are added: close friendship, romantic appeal and job competence.

Adults' self-esteem tends to be based less on intellectual factors and more on areas associated with home, work and family, such as sociability, morality, adequacy as a partner and a provider and so on.

The child has a unique view of himself or herself based largely on the messages he or she gets from the significant others in his or her life. It follows that if these messages are negative or derogatory the child will begin to have a negative view of himself or herself. Perhaps you can recall the times you have heard negative messages given to children by adults or other children:

'You're stupid.'
'You're a thicko.'
'You're too slow.'
'You don't listen to a word I say.'
'You're a bully.'
'You are the worst child I've ever dealt with.'
'You are worse than your sister and she was bad.'
'You little ****. Don't you ever do that again!'
'We don't want you in our group.'

You know how uncomfortable it feels, even as a listener, so how much more it can hurt if it is personally directed. You probably have experiences in your own childhood when you remember being berated or put down. Such experiences stay with us and can hurt for quite a time after the event.

No teacher or assistant or parent is perfect and there are times when things are said which are regretted. However, it is only when the child consistently and regularly hears bad messages about himself or herself that he starts to believe what he hears. It is therefore very important that we consider carefully the words we use with the children we work with.

I was once in a classroom observing an eight year old girl whose name was Samantha. In watching the lesson, I made a point of recording what the teacher said to her at intervals when interaction took place. This is what the teacher said:

> 'You haven't written your name in the right place.'
> 'You haven't been listening to what I've been saying.'
> 'Put your hand down. You shouldn't be asking me for that information. It's on the board.'
> 'You know we don't use pen to draw the margin.'
> 'You're not looking at the board.'
> 'I've said it three times. You're not paying attention.'
> (*Note all the negative comments in this 'teacher talk'*)

By this stage Samantha had got the message and was asking to go to the toilet. I guess it seemed like a better option!

Let's look at some examples of adult language in the classroom and see how we can use the same number of words to give the same meaning in a much more positive frame, and will give a much more upbeat feel to the relationship:

NEGATIVE	POSITIVE
'Don't do that'	'Come and do this'
'Stop messing about'	'Get on with your work'
'You haven't listened'	'Listen to me'
'You can't go out until you've finished your work'	'You can go out as soon as your work is finished'
'Stop running in the corridor'	'Walk in the corridor'
'You're not looking at the book'	'Look at the book'

As you will see, negative messages don't really seem to move things on but just serve to make children feel worse. On the other hand you can give a better message which is much more upbeat, and which gives a clear direction. It also clarifies what behaviour is wanted rather than what is not wanted.

Self-esteem and learning

There is an interesting relationship between self-esteem and learning and by learning, I am referring to both learning the curriculum *and* learning good behaviour.

Research has been done which demonstrates that self-esteem affects the way we view ourselves as learners. When given a task to do, people with low self-esteem who complete it correctly tend to attribute their success to EXTERNAL factors saying things like 'The task was too easy' or 'That was a piece of luck'. If they cannot complete the task they attribute this to EXTERNAL factors saying 'The task was too hard' or 'The teacher hasn't explained it properly'. They may then go on to relate failure to their own failings.

However, people with positive self-esteem, when they complete a task successfully attribute their success to INTERNAL or self-behavioural factors and tend to say (or think) 'I worked really hard' or 'I'm clever'. If they cannot do the task then their reaction is 'I will have to learn how to do that' or 'If I try a bit harder, I will probably get it right'.

If a pupil with low self-esteem is criticised for inappropriate behaviour he or she is likely to respond by saying 'It's not fair' or 'It is not my fault' whereas a pupil with positive self-esteem would tend to say 'Well it's because I did something wrong'. It seems to be too risky for pupils who feel bad about themselves to admit to getting things wrong.

In fact most people, if blamed for something, have strong feelings of denial and aggression at first but those with a positive self-esteem are better able to rationalise the treatment and 'bounce back'. So it is more likely that pupils with low self-esteem will show more aggressive behaviour than those who feel OK about themselves. A vicious circle is set up as shown in Figure 3.1:

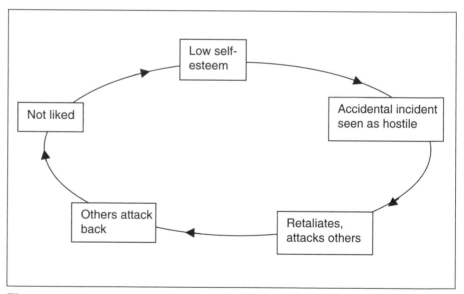

Figure 3.1 The vicious circle of low self-esteem

I observed this behaviour recently in a classroom and you may have observed this sort of thing too. John, a boy with low self-esteem was leaning back on his chair with his bag dangling behind. Another boy walked by and accidentally tripped over John's bag. John was immediately on the offensive, he turned round and swore at the boy. This caused a verbal reaction, which, had the teacher not intervened, could have ended up as a fight.

John saw this act as a deliberate offence against himself and his space. Most other pupils would be able to let the incident pass without comment, but those with low self-esteem are often quick to anger and retaliate, taking the incident personally.

As an assistant your job is to try to break this cycle by boosting the self-esteem of the child so they are less likely to view incidents as hostile and thus becomes less likely to retaliate.

Some signs of low self-esteem

Disparaging remarks about oneself.
Boastfulness.
Being very timid in new situations.
Avoiding stressful situations.
Trying to avoid the possibility of failure (e.g. by not attempting a task).
Continually asking for reassurance.
Being apathetic in learning situations.
Blaming others or circumstances for failure ('It's not my fault because ...').
Reluctance to take responsibility.
Distrusting others but at the same time being desperate to be liked.
Being very reluctant to make decisions, preferring to let others take the responsibility.

Why does self-esteem matter?

There has been a lot of research done on self-esteem. A brief summary of the findings is as follows:

- Children with poor self-esteem are not as able to change their behaviour. Since they feel they are not going to succeed at the task anyway, why bother?
- Children with poor self-esteem try to avoid situations where they may fail and are therefore reluctant to learn. Learning is risky, they may get it wrong.
- Improving their self-esteem therefore means they are more likely to 'have a go' at the task and are thus more likely to learn.
- An improvement in self-esteem tends to mean that children start to believe that their own behaviour can change and once they believe their behaviour can change, it is actually more likely to.
- Children with high self-esteem tend to be educationally and psychologically much more effective and they achieve more.
- Many children with special educational needs have low self-esteem in addition to their educational or behavioural problems.

In the document *National Curriculum and its Assessment* Sir Ron Dearing said:

Education is not only concerned with equipping pupils with the knowledge and skills they need to earn a living, it must help our young people to: use leisure time creatively, have respect for other people's cultures and beliefs, become good citizens, think things out for themselves and last, but not least, value themselves and their achievements.

How can I help to raise self-esteem?

The first step in helping children to develop a more positive self-image involves:

- Defining the child's present strengths and,
- building on them step-by-step.

To do this successfully children need to understand what each task is about and how to do it so success is possible.

The following checklist can help the pupil, and you, as you work together:

Pupil checklist:

- Do I know what this task is about?
- Do I know how to go about it?
- Can I see what the end of this task is?
- Am I going to be able to complete this task?
- If I can complete it, can I do so without looking silly?

Assistant checklist (to ask the pupil):

- What is the task?
- How are you going to do it?
- How long will it take?
- What are the difficult parts?
- What are you likely to need help with?

Assistant checklist (after the task):

- Was it as hard as you thought?
- Which bits were difficult?
- Did it take as long as you thought?
- Why do you think that you were able to do it?

Here are some ideas which will help in building the self-esteem of the pupils you work with:

Working one-to-one with the pupil

- Label the behaviour and not the pupil.
- Prevention is better than cure: intervene early.
- Give feedback sensitively.
- Be respectful.
- Use non-verbal techniques appropriately (smile!).
- Organise the activity so that the pupil knows they can succeed at the task.
- When possible, involve the pupil in planning if an individualised programme is being run.
- Build on any expertise the pupil has.
- Try to get to know the pupil as a person. Find out about their interests.
- Give them the chance to get to know you as a person. Share your interests.

- Be prepared to 'take the risk yourself' (i.e. if a pupil is not coping it may be the work set is too hard. 'Sorry that work I set was too hard. Let me try again').
- Act as a positive model yourself.
- Have positive expectation within realistic limits.
- Give constructive feedback about work.
- Give constructive feedback about behaviour.
- Encourage and reinforce positive self-statements.
- Encourage positive statements about others.
- Encourage the child to work on their own, without your support.
- Allow the safe expression of feelings.
- Adopt a mediation policy that allows all views to be heard.
- Try to ease the fear of failure.
- Specifically remind pupils of past successes.
- Reinforce the idea that success is due to effort rather than just being clever.
- Know what is a reasonable expectation for the pupil.
- Do not put pupils in situations where they are bound to fail.
- Acknowledge pupil's feelings.
- Attribute failure, when appropriate, to external factors.

Working with the pupil in the group or class

- Give positive acknowledgement of any responses made by the pupil, even inappropriate or challenging responses can be channelled into a more appropriate frame of behaviour. Positive responses to the pupil will encourage the others in the group to think positively about the him or her.
- Provide individual instruction to the pupil with gradual weaning to reduce the reliance on support.
- Demonstrate the pupil's successes to convince him/her that success is already being achieved and that further success is possible.
- Persuade the pupil to attempt to work where failure may be a necessary component in the learning process and to realise that everyone experiences failure.
- Provide opportunities for increased participation, e.g. giving the pupil responsibility, working firstly with one partner (possibly weaker) and then gradually increasing the size of the group.
- Encourage the pupil to help with younger less able children.
- Encourage the pupil to attempt a response before offering guidance or offering solutions.
- Establish with the group that everybody's opinions are valid because there is frequently more than one answer.
- Encourage a range of responses to problems.
- Praise or accept unusual responses. Avoid responding negatively to a pupil's suggestions.
- If possible, plan for changes in a supportive way. Prepare the pupil to adapt to changes positively, e.g. What if ... ? sessions.
- Devise group work and encourage positive statements and compliments. Discuss the value of criticism and how it can be used.

- Encourage self-evaluation of work, self-correction of drafts. Follow up work after initial marking by the teacher. Encourage self-assessment of performance and anticipation of teacher's comments and grades.
- Encourage the pupil to take responsibility for the outcome of performance and to realise improvement is not only possible but within their power.
- Ensure that every pupil has examples of work displayed.
- Encourage the teacher to notice the pupil's positives (regardless of unappealing habits or appearance, e.g. greeting the pupil and saying goodbye, smiling, etc.)

Activities to improve self-esteem

Here are some practical ideas which you can use to raise self-esteem with the pupils you work with. They will clearly need to be amended in the light of the particular circumstances with any given pupil or group depending on the age of the pupil.

A success a day

At the end of each day, pupils share a success they have had during that day. Pupils with low self-esteem will find this very difficult at first, reporting that they have had no successes.

You may therefore need to remind such pupils during the day when there is some minor triumph that this could count as their success: answering a question, completing a piece of work, having someone to play with at break – all of these could, for some children, be successes which children with low self-esteem tend not to recognise.

With some groups it may be appropriate for them to write (or dictate) a sentence about their success that day. This would build into a cumulative record which can be used to 'prove' to the pupil that they are making progress.

Positive pictures (for younger children)

Talk with pupils about how easy it is to 'put someone down'. Discuss that there is always good to be found in everybody if we look.

Using big paper, draw around two or three children's bodies. At some time of the day, have the rest of the class dictate or write something positive about the selected children. Put the positive sentences up attached to the drawings. Repeat so that over a reasonably short length of time everybody has had positive comments displayed.

On my mind

A follow-up or more 'grown-up' variant on the above. Draw (or have the pupils draw) a large profile or silhouette of their head. Then write or cut out of newspapers, etc. words which express some of their current concerns.

This activity works towards legitimising the private thoughts of each pupil and can help people to realise that they are not alone in many of their concerns, making them feel more 'normal'.

Special day

A large sign is put on the class-room door 'Today is (child's name) day!' Each child in turn gets his or her name on the door. Everybody has to do all they can to make it a good day for that particular child. *Variant:* Pupil of the week. Each week draw two pupils' names out of a box. The others have to state what they like about the chosen pupils: try to get between 6 to 10 statements, keeping them about the same length for each child.

Quickies

Sitting in a circle ask the children to say something in or out of school that they are good at (children with low self-esteem will need warning of this and perhaps need some help so they have a contribution to make – otherwise this could be very threatening!).

Get the pupils to write a paragraph about something they would like to change about themselves. Ensure they know the difference between things which could be changed (even if only in theory) and things which can't.

Pictures or stories illustrating 'something I am proud of'.

Pictures or stories illustrating 'the nicest thing I ever did' and 'the nicest thing that somebody did for me'.

Lottery fantasy: they have won £2 million in the lottery – but they can only have it if they give £1 million away. What would they do with it, and why?

Names

Have the pupils look up what their names mean. (If they have an unusual name that is not listed in the usual sources, make sure you explain that this is because their name is really special, and suggest they ask their parents how their name was chosen or created.) *Questions:* What function do names serve? Who decides what name a person gets? Where do names come from? What about nicknames? Have them invent a positive nickname for themselves (or each other) based on some genuine personal attributes or something from their personal history. This can obviously lead into further sessions on name-calling and the feelings that evokes.

Positive feelings

Get the class or a group to share something that somebody has done that made them feel happy. Ask them to explain why it gave them a good feeling. *Variant:* Get them to talk about something they have done which they think made someone else feel good.

Positive feedback

At the end of small group sessions, pupils can be encouraged to give each other positive feedback. Beginning statements include: 'I liked it when you...' 'It helped me when you...' 'We were better as a group today because you...'. Obviously as an assistant you need to model this sort of behaviour on a regular basis.

Positive support

Ask each child to list, and later share, five things that another person can do to recognise that their contribution was useful. For example, smile at me, listen while I talk, tell me that you missed me when I wasn't here, tell me my contribution was useful and so on. Again it is important for the assistant to model this sort of behaviour.

What if...

Ask the pupil to pretend that one of their possessions could talk. Ask 'What might it say good about you?' *Examples:* bed; bike; pet; school desk; coat; shoes; ball; doll, etc.

Ask 'If you were an animal, what animal would you be and why?' This can lead on to discussion about positive qualities.

I used to be...but now...

If the children do this verbally, each child has to think of something that has changed as they have got older, thus reinforcing the idea that things can change. For children with low self-esteem it can be helpful to ask them (or others) 'What did you do that helped or caused this change?' If they do the same exercise in writing, their responses can be cut up and mounted in a random order as part of a display about 'growing up' or 'things we have changed'.

Weekly reaction sheets

Part of enhancing pupil's self-concept is helping them to become more aware of the control that they do have over their day-to-day life. Filling out weekly reaction sheets can help pupils to see how effectively they are using their time. Example questions might be:

What was the high point of the week?

What could you have done to make the week better?

What could somebody else have done?

Identify three choices you made this week – what were their results?

Did you make any plans for anything you will do next week?

The adult then reviews the sheet with the pupil, giving appropriate feedback.

The goalposts

Have a set of 'goalposts' on a wall. Each day (or week) allow pupils to set themselves a 'target' written on a circular index card (the ball). When it is reached the card is moved within the goalposts – the pupil has scored a 'goal'. They share it and how they completed the goal with the class at an appropriate time. Those who do not complete their goals simply have their cards taken down – they do not have to explain why they weren't reached. Some youngsters may obviously need some assistance in forming realistic targets!

They should be taught that targets should be realistic, achievable, desirable, and measurable. This is a powerful technique in that it can make accomplishments that are often overlooked very explicit.

I am not my description

Many children when asked to describe themselves will put down generalised negative labels like 'bad', 'naughty', 'stupid'. If such labels are collected from a group they can be put up and then discussed along the following lines: 'Are people always bad?' 'Under what circumstances are people bad?' Help the children to realise that such descriptors are just labels which are attached to certain sorts of (undesirable) behaviours, not fixed personality characteristics.

Show them how to rewrite their 'bad' words to make them more realistic and less damaging to themselves. This means writing or talking about specific behaviours in specific situations: 'Yesterday I hit Peter' rather than 'I am a bad person'. This then leads into individual or group discussions about alternative actions the person could have taken. However, if it is not appropriate to personalise it, there can be discussion about bad/good, for example, being the ends of a continuum rather than opposites.

To go back to our original analogy, there are many activities during the school day which allow you to put 'money in the child's pocket'. Take every opportunity you can to do this and you will begin to see the results. Remember that every interaction you have with the child, both verbal and non-verbal, will be interpreted as valuing or devaluing and will affect his or her self-esteem.

Most children will begin to flourish using these approaches but because of adverse home circumstances, some will find it harder. Don't give up! As adults people remember those significant others in their childhood who had faith in them and provided consistent encouragement and care.

KEY POINT

Overnight changes are unlikely! It has taken a long time for the child to get to their present point and it may take some time for positive changes to be seen – so don't give up.

ACTION BOX

You can try this yourself:
Listen to your own use of words when talking with children and see if you can change some of the negative messages you might use into positives. You will be amazed what a difference it makes! Your non-verbal behaviour can also affect the child's self-esteem – eyebrows raised, 'tut-tutting', shaking the head, turning away when speaking to the child – all these non-verbals convey messages too so be aware of the importance of this and try to give smiles, nods, pats on the back, thumbs up or whatever feels comfortable in conveying positive regard for the child.

Chapter 4

Describing, observing and recording behaviour

In the course of your work with children and young people who have behaviour difficulties you will find that if you step back from working directly with the child and become a 'fly on the wall' you will get a lot of information about what is going on that will add to your understanding of what is causing the behaviour to occur. In practice, it is quite difficult to do this because in your normal role you will be very much engaged in conversation and interactions with a number of pupils and, should you choose to do an observation, you will be approached for help unrelentingly unless you make it clear that you are 'unavailable'. You need to tell the pupils that they are to pretend that you are not there because you have to do an important job of watching the whole class and are not allowed to speak! Once you have managed to persuade members of the class not to approach you, you will be ready to do an observation of classroom behaviour.

Where should I start?

The first step is, of course, to negotiate the observation with the class teacher so that he or she is aware of the purpose of what you propose and willing for you to do this. Before starting an observation of behaviour it is helpful to have an idea of what behaviours you might want to observe and what words or phrases you might use to describe the behaviour you see.

What might I want to observe?

There are a number of areas of child behaviour that you might want to investigate. You might do this by observing:

- How much time a child spends 'on task', i.e. doing what they are supposed to be doing.
- What the child's attitude to learning is, e.g. whether he or she starts the task straight away or shows some 'avoidance' behaviour.
- How much the child interacts with other children, e.g. starts conversations (or not), responds to other children appropriately, cooperates in group activities, etc.
- How a child plays, e.g. concentration on one activity or flitting between activities.
- How well the child responds to teacher directions, i.e. whether he or she responds straight away or has to be reminded.

- How much attention the teacher has to give to the child.
- How much teacher attention the child demands.
- How much time the child spends in his or her seat.
- How much work the child produces compared with most of the others in the class.
- How the child is influenced (or not) by children around him or her.
- Whether the child seems restless, e.g. showing rocking or fidgeting behaviour.
- Whether the child has learned anything by the end of the lesson.

There are some general impressions you will get as you observe the pupil. These will be about whether he or she seems happy or unhappy, settled or unsettled. Also about whether he or she is included as part of activities by others or excluded and how much time the teacher spends on the child relative to the others in the group. Observation often tells you a lot about teacher behaviour too and it will be a very useful exercise to share your findings with the teacher after the observation (this can sometimes be a learning experience for the teacher!).

What words or phrases might be useful?

When you start to describe behaviour, it is really helpful if you can be clear in your descriptions so that people reading what you have written know exactly what you observed. Many statements about behaviour are not absolutely clear, e.g. 'He is disruptive' gives an idea of a boy who is posing some behaviour problem but it doesn't really tell us anything and we don't know what it is he is doing. It would be clearer if we were to say 'He shouts out frequently'. We call descriptions which are not clear 'fuzzies' and we try to avoid them if possible in our descriptions of behaviour. One way of judging whether a statement about behaviour is fuzzy or clear is to apply the 'Hey dad' test.

This works as follows: Take any statement about behaviour and if you can preface it by the words 'Hey dad, come and watch me...' and it seems to make sense, then it is clear. If it does not make sense then it is a fuzzy.

Tony pushed Ed in the corridor

So for example 'Hey dad, come and watch me 'showing antisocial behaviour' is fuzzy, as we do not know what is going on and it sounds silly. However 'Hey dad, come and watch me tearing Mark's book up' is clear – we know exactly what is happening! As you practise describing behaviours you will get better at avoiding fuzzy terms and become more focused in your descriptions.

How shall I record what I observe?

There are a number of different ways to record your observations of behaviour. It helps if you can start with a framework for recording which will help you to analyse what you have seen.

Ongoing observation   This is the simplest of all observation formats when you will be jotting down significant things you notice in the order in which they happen. It provides a 'running commentary' of what the pupil was doing so that the reader has a pretty good idea of the general behaviour of the pupil in the lesson. It is really helpful following an observation done in this way if you can record the 'issues arising from the observation' at the end.

Name: Katie G   *Date:* 3 June 2001
Lesson: Maths   *Time:* 10–10.30 a.m.

K. comes into the classroom and sits by J. Teacher asks class to get out their maths books. K. gets up and moves to her tray. On the way she talks to P. K. takes a long time to find her book. Teacher asks her to hurry up. K. does not do this. K. then finds her book and returns to her seat. She starts rocking on her chair and the teacher tells her to sit still. K's group is asked to listen to the teacher who explains the task. K. does not appear to be listening. The group start the task. K. writes the date at the top of the page then reaches over to borrow J's rubber. J. takes his rubber from K. and K. protests. K. complains to the teacher that J. has taken his rubber back. The teacher brings a rubber for K. to use and asks her to get on with the maths. K. says she doesn't know how to do it and the teacher explains the first sum then moves away. K. gazes around her and gets up from her chair to sharpen her pencil at the back of the class. She stares out of the window. The teacher asks K. to return to her seat. K. does so. K. puts her hand up and asks if she can go to the toilet.

Issues arising from observation

- K. finds it hard to settle to work.
- K. does not seem to get on well with J.
- K. has done no written maths in this lesson.
- K. did not listen to the teacher or understand the teacher's explanation.

In analysing this kind of record you will notice a number of areas to work on with Katie. How to get her to settle to work, where she might sit to avoid distraction, how you might follow up the teachers instructions and explanations, etc.

Time sampling of behaviour   In this kind of observation you will need a format which has timed intervals and you will record the pupil's behaviour by noting what he or she is doing at time intervals, e.g. each minute. You do not record the behaviours in between.

Name: Mark B	Lesson: Science	Date 3: June 2001
	Task: To draw a picture of a caterpillar	
Time	**Behaviour**	
10.01	On task	
10.02	On task	
10.03	Talking to R.	
10.04	On task	
10.05	Out of seat	
10.06	On task	
10.07	Poking C. with his pencil	
10.08	Talking to S.	
10.09	Out of seat	
10.10	Under table looking for pencil	

This kind of observation helps you to estimate how much time Mark spent doing what he was supposed to be doing. As he was 'on task' for 4 out of 10 observations, you might conclude that this means that for 40 per cent of his time he is working and for 60 per cent of his time he is not. You might also conclude that he spends time talking to others when he shouldn't be so you then might think of ways to help him to work without distracting others.

Event sampling of behaviour   For this kind of observation you will have decided which behaviours you want to observe and will record the number of times these behaviours occur within a specific time frame, e.g. it is a useful way of testing your theories about what might be happening or finding out which behaviours are actually causing most disruption.

Name: Robert T	Lesson: Literacy Hour	Date: 3 June 2001	
		Time: 10–10.30 a.m.	
Time	**Calling out**	**Out of seat**	**On task**
10.00–10.05	3	2	3 mins
10.05–10.10	2	0	2 mins
10.10–10.15	2	1	1 min
10.15–10.20	0	0	0 min
10.20–10.25	0	1	4 mins
10.25–10.30	2	2	2 mins
TOTAL	9	6	12/30

Looking at this analysis, you might feel that a good place to start work would be to reduce Robert's 'calling out' behaviour, as this is what he does most.

What did I find out from the observation?

There are a number of useful questions which you need to ask yourself about what you have observed. These are as follows:

Did the child learn much in the lesson?	Yes/No
How was the child learning?	Independently? A directed activity? Adult directed? No learning observed.
Did the child appear to be	Confident? Interested? Involved? Enjoying the lesson?
Did the child cooperate with	The teacher? The assistant? The others in the class?

In making your analysis it will be helpful to consider the following questions:

- What does this observation tell you about the child's interests, experience, skills, attitudes and knowledge?
- Does this information indicate improvement, deterioration or a change of attitude?
- What are the main causes for concern?

Whatever observation techniques you use, the key question at the end of this process is:

- *How am I going to use the information I have gained from observing as a basis for planning the next step in the child's learning and behaviour?*

It is very important that you discuss your ideas with the class teacher or SENCO.

ACTION BOX

Have a look at the following statements and try to decide which are clear and which are fuzzy.
1. She has complained about bullying three times this week.
2. He is a major disruptive element in class.
3. She misses a geography lesson every week.
4. He shows no interest at all in my lessons.
5. He stays behind in class every playtime, unless I move him out.
6. He's a shy boy. I don't think he'll ever speak up in class.
7. She stole items from the teacher's desk on four occasions last term.
8. He is an aggressive character, often pushing others about.

(Answers on page 100)

Chapter 5

Behaviour management: a framework for understanding where to start

As we have seen in the previous chapter, it is important to gather information about the pupil's behaviour in order to make a plan for behaviour management which is going to be effective. Once we think we know what the problems are, how do we start to plan for change?

There are a number of ways of working with children and young people which will affect their behaviour and these tend to fall into two groups.

'Inside out' strategies

There are ways of working which attempt to change the child's internal view about himself or herself and the result is better behaviour. Some examples of 'inside out' approaches are play therapy, psychotherapy, counselling, cognitive behaviour therapy and psychoanalysis. These therapeutic techniques require skilled training and are usually delivered over several sessions. These approaches tend to be used more with adults although some teenagers, especially those with depression or eating disorders, benefit from this sort of intervention. Later in this book we will look at how to use active listening as a tool for supporting children and young people with behaviour difficulties. This is also an 'inside out' approach.

'Outside in' strategies

These are ways of working which start by changing the external factors which affect a child's behaviour, e.g. the environment, the rules, the rewards used, etc. As a result, a change in the child's behaviour may lead to changes in the way he or she views himself or herself. It has been clearly demonstrated in the behaviour experiments carried out by social psychologists that human behaviour can change by changing the environment and conditions.

It is usually the 'outside in' approaches we use in schools, as most schools do not have access to on-site counsellors. It is also rare to find psychologists or psychotherapists giving 'inside out' ongoing support in schools.

Whatever approach is used, it is important to remember the following key point.

> **KEY POINT**
>
> For behaviour change to occur you, as the adult in the relationship, must make the first moves.

The pupil is not going to wake up one morning and think 'Well I'm going to change my behaviour today', it just doesn't happen. So it is up to the parent, the therapist, the teacher or the assistant to be the one to change something first.

In psychotherapy practice, there is a notion of 'family scripts' and you will be familiar with this phenomenon. The theory is that in any family or relationship there develops a way of interacting within which all parties are trying to get their needs met. In arguments the family members tend to say the same sorts of things and react to each other in such a way as if they were following a script, in that each disagreement tends to have the same sort of progression and outcome. Individual members of the family react in 'predictable' ways and get stuck in the same cul-de-sacs each time. It is like standing dominoes in a circle and knocking one over, sure enough all the other dominoes will topple, they can be stood up and the same domino can be knocked over – and of course the same pattern happens. It is like this with interactions or 'scripts'. The same sorts of things are said and the same sorts of things happen. It is clearly necessary for this pattern to be changed or broken in some way before the predictable results can be changed.

It happens every playtime, she just never seems to learn

So if you want the behaviour of a pupil you are working with to change, then it is you, as the adult in the relationship, who must be pro-active in doing something different.

Following on from the work of behaviourist psychologists, there was considerable interest in 'behaviour modification' which evolved into an approach which advocated 'praise the good and ignore the bad'. Since then, this has been refined and developed into an extended and more useful framework:

1. **Change the environment.**
2. **Teach new skills.**
3. **Reinforce good behaviour.**
4. **Plan reactive strategies.**

We need to consider each of these four components as we plan to manage behaviour, whether we are working with just one child, a group or the whole class. Let's explore these areas in greater detail.

1. Change the environment

Why might we want to do this? We all behave differently in different environments but some pupils find it difficult to adapt their behaviour appropriately to alternative environments. We might need to help them to do this. When the child is in school he or she is responding to a range of influences. Figure 5.1 is helpful in demonstrating this:

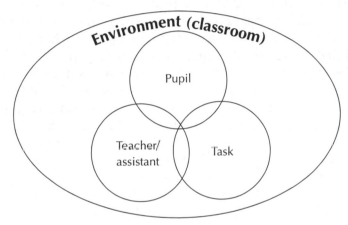

Figure 5.1 Interacting influences in the classroom

If we were to change any one of the influences then it might affect the pupil's behaviour. What could we change? Here are some suggestions: Consider the physical environment:

- Is it too hot/too cold?
- Is it too noisy/too quiet?
- Is the room too big/too crowded?
- Is the child's chair at the right height?
- Do they have the right equipment?

Consider the location of the child in the classroom:

- Is he/she sitting close enough to the teacher?
- Does the arrangement of desks/teacher suit the child?
- Is equipment easy to access?

Consider the influence of other pupils:

- Is the child sitting by someone who will distract him/her?
- Is the child sitting by someone who they will distract?
- Is the child sitting too close to others?
- Is the child sitting too far away from others?

Consider the effects of the task:

- Is it too hard/too easy?
- Does the child need support in order to do it?
- Does the child have the necessary equipment to hand?

Consider the effects of the teacher/assistant on the child:

- Are instructions clear?
- Is there enough encouragement?
- Is there frequent checking?
- Is there positive feedback?

Do any of the above factors need to be changed so as to enable the pupil to behave better?

2. Teach new skills

The second component of the framework is the direct teaching of those skills the pupil needs to function effectively, both as a learner and as a socially acceptable member of the class. When children start school we should not assume that they already know how to behave in a group. Most will have been to a preschool playgroup or nursery so will have had some experience of the routines which need to be followed. However, there remain some children who find it difficult to conform to normally expected behaviours in the classroom and this group often need to be taught the behaviours they need in order to help them to belong to the group. It is easy to tell children which behaviours we do not want but is harder to say what behaviours we *do* want. We need to help children to replace inappropriate behaviours with appropriate behaviours, e.g. What does David need to learn to do *instead* of shouting out? – He could learn to put his hand up.

How wil I know what skills to teach?

If you use the ideas for pupil observation given in Chapter 4 then you will have a very clear idea of what behaviours are getting in the way of the child's learning and relationships and, from this analysis, you will know which skills the child lacks, e.g. ability to sit quietly, ability to line up without a fuss, ability to work without distracting others, etc.

How do I do this?

When routines or behaviours are being established, they need to be taught and practised. The following steps are helpful:

- Be clear what the outcome should be.
- Model/demonstrate an example of what is wanted (you can do this or get another pupil to do it).
- Model/demonstrate an example of what *isn't* wanted.
- Get the pupil to identify the 'correct' example.
- Give the pupil opportunities to practise the new skills.
- Highlight the carrying out of the skill in 'real life'.

Chapter 8 gives examples of how specific skills can be taught.

Let me show you how to put your hand up rather than shouting out

3. Reinforcement

Reinforcing good/appropriate behaviour is the third component of the framework and it is crucial to success in managing behaviour. Research has shown that children's behaviour can be *controlled* by hostility and 'the big stick' approach. However, *the key to changing behaviour is the positive reinforcement (rewarding) of what is wanted*. This has frequently been described as 'catch them being good'. If the pupil knows what to do and how to do it but still does not respond as needed, then it is important to have some form of reward or positive reinforcement in order to motivate the pupil to behave. It is human nature to seek external rewards as a result of certain behaviours. Think of how motivating a pay cheque is at the end of each month!

Learning theory tells us that if something we see as pleasant happens as a result of our actions we are inclined to repeat it. Conversely, if something negative happens, we are less likely to repeat it. So, for instance, if you are wearing a particular item of clothing and someone whose opinion you value comments that you look good/younger/slimmer/better in that then you are quite likely to wear it again!

However, if you get negative feedback (and this might include being ignored – no one noticing.) then you are less likely to give that item of clothing many more outings.

Figure 5.2 helps us to understand how this works:

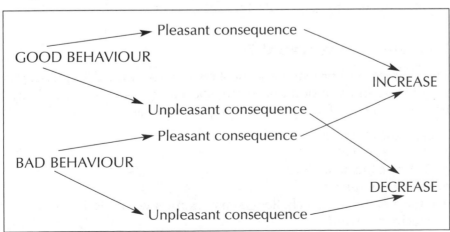

Figure 5.2 Rewards and punishments

What do I need to know about rewards?

There are a number of questions which you need to ask in order to decide which are effective rewards:

* *Is the reward really a reward?*
  That is, is it considered a reward by *the pupil*, not just by you or the teacher. Also, rewards can become overused or 'formula' and therefore lose their effect. You may therefore need to review the rewards you are using and change them fairly frequently.
* *Are you using the reward consistently?*
  There is nothing worse than being promised a carrot then getting a stick! Consistency is so important – if you have said there will be a reward, do remember to deliver and to give the reward consistently especially in the early stages of trying to change behaviour.
* *Do all pupils get rewarded regardless of ability?*
  If we look at research we find that pupils who achieve more get more praise, more questions and more opportunities to respond than pupils who are not good learners. You will need to check that you are giving all the children you work with equal access to encouragement and rewards.
* *Is the reward immediate enough?*
  The most effective rewards are given immediately after good behaviour and the younger the child is the more important this is because young children cannot usually carry the notion of time and may not associate the reward with the behaviour if there is too much time in between.

  However, older pupils will be better able to wait, but don't leave it too long! 'Jam tomorrow' can lose its appeal, particularly for impulsive children. Immediate rewards are particularly important for children with a diagnosis of Attention Deficit/Hyperactivity Disorder (AD/HD).
* *Does the pupil know what they are being rewarded for?*
  When you give a reward it is really important that you remind the child what he or she has done well. 'Well done John, I like the way you have worked quietly.' This confirms the rules which are in operation (in this case, to work quietly) both for the individual and for the others in the group.
* *Is the reward used appropriately?*
  This means matching the level of the reward with the level of achievement. It is useful to have a range of rewards to use which you will need to agree with the class teacher.

What are effective rewards?

The simplest and probably the most effective of rewards is *praise*. It is easy to use and you don't need any special equipment – you always have it with you! This is how to use praise to best effect:

* Gain the child's attention.
* Show approval.
* Describe the behaviour.
* Refer to frequency.
* Give a motivational challenge (and express your confidence).
* Specify a reward.

So, for example, 'Katy, I like the way you have got on well with Emma today. Well done. That's the second time I have noticed you working together. Let's try and make it three times in a row tomorrow. When you've done that, then you can choose an activity after break.' Of course there is not always time to give such a full praise statement but if you can be specific about the praise then it is more effective, e.g. 'Robert, I like the way you came into the classroom today', 'Penny, you have kept your hands to yourself all the lesson. Well done!'

Positive messages do not always need to be verbal, they can also be non-verbal or written. Some simple non-verbal messages are a smile, a nod or a wink. A pat on the back or a handshake can also be effective body language. Written rewards can be quite powerful, a positive comment on a piece of work or a post-it note with a good news message can be really effective. Most effective of all is a positive note sent home or a telephone call to parents/carers to share some good news about the child – you need to check with the teacher you work with about whether you are able to do this.

Tangible rewards

Young children love stickers or smiley face stamps either to wear or stick on their work. Children not so young also find these motivating. Some schools now have school keyrings, pens or mugs which can be used as rewards for consistent achievement in behaviour or doing well in learning. In the chapter on managing the difficult behaviour of individual children, you will find some ideas for rewards.

Consequences of bad/inappropriate behaviours

We do need some sanctions or punishments to fall back on when other strategies are not working. However, you do need to be careful about the use of punishment because it can be reinforcing of bad behaviours if it results in attention. This is why it is so important that, in general, the pupil gets *more* rewards for appropriate behaviour than punishments for poor behaviour.

Sanctions and punishments are given with the aim of preventing the bad behaviour happening again, they suppress poor behaviour but do not teach appropriate behaviour. Sometimes they can be damaging and humiliating. You can probably remember examples from your own school days when you or another member of your class was publicly humiliated and how that made you feel.

One head teacher tells a tale of his school days recounting the fact that he had played as a member of the school football team in the final and the team had lost. As a result the team was caned by the head teacher in front of the whole school! It seems hardly credible nowadays and yet such things occurred. Such incidents serve to make situations worse rather than better. Do you think the team players would be more or less likely to want to play for the school team as a result of that punishment?

The effect of giving a pupil negative feedback in front of the whole group usually has the effect of lowering their self-esteem and is unlikely to produce the permanent effect of positive behaviour change.

If sanctions or punishments are to be used effectively the following questions need to be asked:

- *Is the punishment really a punishment?*
  We need to be sure that the sanction is indeed a negative consequence for the pupil and not a positive consequence.

  Telling a child to stay in at breaktime to finish work would be a real punishment for most but for some it may be quite a pleasant alternative to coping with the demands of breaktime. Sometimes negative messages from the adult are attention getting!
- *Is the punishment applied consistently?*
  This is really important. If you give the pupil the choice of behaving well or receiving a sanction and the pupil chooses to behave poorly you must follow through. Punishments become totally ineffective if they are promised then not carried through.

However, along with this we need to remember a key point, i.e. that the punishment needs to be as mild as possible and applied consistently.

KEY POINT

It is not severity of the punishment – it is the consistency with which it is applied that makes it effective.

There should be some flexibility in punishments to take account of individual circumstances, for instance, it would not be helpful informing the parents of some relatively minor misdemeanour if it meant the child would be punished at home as well.

- *Is the punishment immediate enough?*
  Punishment is most effective if it is given soon after the unwanted incident. A *warning* is usually the best first step in this process.
- *Does the pupil know what they are being punished for?*
  Any punishment is more effective if you give a clear explanation of what rule has been broken and what behaviour is expected in the future.

  The focus should be on the behaviour not on the child so you need to depersonalise any critical comment, e.g. 'You must stay behind and finish the work you have not done', NOT 'You are a lazy boy who never gets anything done in my group!'
- *Does the punishment fit the crime?*
  Just as we need a menu of rewards, we also need a range of sanctions which we can use. 'Good' punishments are ones which enable the pupil to repair some of the damage they have caused, e.g. picking up litter, cleaning graffiti off walls and other surfaces, etc.
- *Is the punishment fair?*
  Pupils do respond to a system which is seen as fair. It is therefore really important to avoid punishing the group for the wrong doing of one or two pupils as this just breeds hostility in some pupils. It is unfair – they don't deserve it, it will be remembered and it leads to poorer group relationships.
- *Have pupils been involved in choosing the sanctions?*
  If pupils as a group are involved in negotiating what the sanction should be, then they are more likely to be effective. It is often

surprising to hear how extreme some pupils would think the sanctions should be – hanging would be too good for some!

- *Is the punishment applied calmly?*
  It is often the case that bad behaviour arouses in us strong emotional reactions. We need to be very careful how we react and STAY CALM. Punishment is more effective for pupils and less stressful for adults if it is applied calmly. You need to control your emotions if you want the pupil to do the same.

The Elton Report (Department of Education and Science 1989) about discipline in schools summarises the effective use of punishment as follows:

- Firm rather than aggressive.
- Targeting the right pupil.
- Criticising the behaviour NOT the person.
- Using private not public reprimands.
- Being fair and consistent.
- Avoiding sarcasm or idle threats.

We could also add:

- Not physically or mentally harmful.
- Not infringing the rights of the child.

What are effective punishments?

In *Assertive Discipline* (Canter and Canter 1992) we are given helpful ideas on punishment (negative consequences). There is a menu of possibilities beginning with a warning. This is an alert to the pupil about their behaviour which is often enough to stop the behaviour from getting worse. If it does not do this then the next negative consequence should be given, usually this is that the child is moved away from the group for a short period but remains in the classroom.

If we remember that children want to 'belong' and dislike being moved away from the group then this strategy can be quite powerful. These two strategies work for the great majority of children. For those who have behaviour which is particularly difficult to manage other strategies beyond these will need to be used (these are described in Chapter 7).

4. Plan reactive strategies

Reactive strategies are rarely necessary if the first three components of the framework have been implemented. Reactive strategies are for crisis management of behaviour, i.e. when things go badly wrong and you have to react swiftly to manage the situation. These situations are really the domain of the teacher and you will normally not be required to manage them. They often involve physical restraint which should only be used in exceptional circumstances and only then with clear planning, training, authorisation and back-up (see p. 103 for more details).

KEY POINT

Behaviour is a response to context – environment, other people or the activity. The child is reacting to these factors. It may be that something in the context needs to change, rather than the child.

Chapter 6

Managing group behaviour: strategies that work

'Group management skills are probably the most important single factor in achieving good standards of classroom behaviour.'
(Department of Education and Science 1989)

As an assistant you are very likely to be asked to work with groups either in-class or outside the classroom under the guidance of the class teacher and you will be usually given a task to supervise. However, new assistants soon find that before you can support the learning process, you have to manage the behaviour of the group so that the children settle down before they can get on with the activity.

Consider what happens when you arrange any group of people around a table – they start to talk – because essentially this arrangement is a social arrangement. For some tasks and activities this may be fine but for others it is not so and you will therefore need strategies which enable you to manage group behaviour so that all the pupils in the group learn as well as possible.

Social psychologists (including Froyen) have identified four stages which groups pass through. Effective teachers and assistants are those who have skills in managing the group through these stages. These are:

Forming   The group starts out together and individuals are 'weighing each other up'. Usually behaviour problems are not significant. At this stage adults need to set the 'ground rules' of what is expected.

Storming   This is the 'testing of the boundaries' stage when individual children begin to act up. Adults need to be clear about what the boundaries are at this stage and consistent with rewards and sanctions.

Norming   Depending on the reaction of the adult at the storming stage, the group settles into an unwritten agreement of what is possible and what is not.

Performing   The group works together cohesively and gets on with learning – but *only* if the first three stages – especially the storming stage, have been managed well.

Do we need rules?

The answer is yes. Reasonable rules are an important part of any social situation and are there to give clarity about what behaviour is expected. It will normally be up to the whole-school staff, working together with governors, parents and pupils to determine what the appropriate rules might be for the school. It is up to the teacher in the classroom to ensure these rules are formed and followed and you will be working under the guidance of the teacher to support pupils in keeping the rules. If you work in a situation where the rules are not explicit and taught by the class teacher, then you may need to discuss this with the class teacher/SENCO. In this case you may have to determine your own rules, the rules you need to use when working with groups of children.

What are effective rules?

A long list of do's and don'ts is not usually helpful, mainly because pupils cannot remember them all (nor can teachers or assistants!). Effective rules are those which are fair, relevant and consistently applied. They should be written down for all to see and should have the following characteristics:

- Clearly worded.
- Positively phrased (e.g. 'walk down the corridors' *not* 'don't run down the corridors').
- Brief and to the point.
- Few in number.
- Teachable and enforceable.
- Apply to everyone.

Examples of 'good' rules:

- Follow the adult's directions.
- No teasing or swearing (this one is hard to phrase positively!).
- Work quietly.
- Be ready to start on time.
- Have all the equipment you need.
- Keep hands and feet to yourself.

Routines

Whether you are able to set rules or not, you will certainly need to be involved in supporting the routines that the teacher establishes for the day-to-day situations which require pupils to behave in certain ways for things to run smoothly, e.g. getting changed for PE, lining up at the door, getting work out of trays, putting it away, etc. Routines are agreed sequences of actions which the adult usually sets and the pupils learn and follow. Sometimes, you may have to plan routines if you are working with groups. Effective routines have the following characteristics:

- They start with a clear signal.
- They are consistent – the same each time.
- They are clear and efficient – they do the job as quickly as possible and the children learn them easily.

You need to teach routines at the start of the school year and when working with a new group – and you will probably need to remind the group quite frequently during the learning period. So, for example, if you want the group to learn to line up at the door, in a line without pushing and shoving or running, you would start with a clear signal which might be saying 'Right, listen everyone' (wait for attention from all).

'When I say, I want you to *walk* to the door and make a line without touching the person in front of you.'

'OK do it now.'

(Remember to give praise when the pupils comply).

Giving directions or instructions

These are specific actions required in specific situations. In the course of any school day you will be giving many directions to the groups you work with. Here are some guidelines to make your directions effective:

- Give a signal that a direction is coming.
- WAIT for attention from the group (eye contact, body position).
- Give a reminder not to start carrying out the instruction until you say so.
- Give any reasons for the activity, *before* the instructions.

and then express the required action:

- Positively.
- Using short clear phrases and avoiding long commands.
- Say when you want the action to begin.

So, for example, if you want the group to use scissors, glue and paper to make a model house, you might say:

'OK everyone, look at me (or listen now). I am going to tell you what you need to make the house.'	Signal
WAIT until all the group are listening. Remind those who don't stop – 'James look at me', 'Gemma, ready?'	WAIT
'I don't want you to touch the scissors or glue before I tell you.'	Remind them not to start before you say
'We are going to make the house like the one we have just seen on TV.'	Give reasons before instructions
'You will be picking up the paper and cutting along the lines. Then you will glue the sides together.'	Positive, clear and simple
'Right, begin now.'	Give a clear message that they can start

One really good tip in giving directions is to remind yourself to keep instructions short and positive, stating what you want the pupil or group to do, e.g:

'I want you to get on with your work.'
'I want you to put your book away.'
'I want you to talk quietly.'

You need to remember that some pupils (often those who are difficult to manage) have very poor short-term memories for verbal instructions so it is important to give instructions or directions in 'bite-sized' pieces to those particular pupils. They just cannot remember a long string of words.

When you start working with a new group they need to learn the rules and routines before they can learn the curriculum and you might need to demonstrate the behaviours you want. The following steps are helpful:

- Define the rule or direction and be sure the pupil understands what is wanted.
- Model or demonstrate how you need things to be done, e.g. 'This is how I want you to sit'. Alternatively you can get one of the pupils to demonstrate how to do it.
- It is then quite helpful (and amusing) to demonstrate how NOT to do it.
- The pupils can then identify good and bad examples.
- Let the pupils practise the routine.
- Praise when it happens in reality!

Teaching rules and routines

It will help the group to work well if you think about the framework discussed in Chapter 5 and how that can be applied to groups.

- **Change the environment.**
- **Teach new skills.**
- **Reinforce good behaviour.**
- **Plan reactive strategies.**

How do I get the group to settle and work together?

When managing a group you need to be particularly aware of this. It will be helpful before you start to think about the seating arrangements. You might decide to have a particular child sitting next to you and you will know only too well which children you will need to separate! You will need to think about whether the group should sit round a table, on the floor or at desks and you will also need to have the equipment you need ready and close by – pencils sharpened, enough paper for everyone, etc. It is also extremely important that you prepare for dealing with the different rates of working of group members so you will need to have ready work which is *differentiated*, i.e. matched to the ability levels of the group. The teacher should help you to do this. It is necessary to avoid pupils becoming bored and 'off task', which is when behaviour problems are likely to occur.

Change the environment

Teach new skills

We have already considered the importance of teaching rules and routines. You need to give the group frequent reminders of the ways you need them to behave so that you can get the work done. With all your approaches try to be successful and you need to remember:

KEY POINT

If it works, do more of it. If it doesn't work, do something different.

Reinforcement

This means giving encouragement and positive feedback to the group when they follow your directions and get on with the activity you are supervising. It is important not to stop the flow of work but you can choose the right moments to give feedback:

'Well done everybody. I like the way you are all working quietly.'

'Daniel and Ben are working well together today, keep it up – really good.'

It is important that the group hears good messages from you early on in the activity as it encourages group members to settle. Try and find something positive to say at an early stage e.g. 'Well done green group – you came in quietly today.'

It is also good to end the session with a positive message to the group. 'You've all done well today and tried hard, I have enjoyed working with you.'

This kind of group praise works well with all age groups although you will have to be sensitive towards the needs of secondary age pupils as specific identification does not always go down well, but do remember to give some positive message to each member of the group if you can.

The week's best pupil

Research into the way teachers use praise with pupils has shown that teachers give three times more positive comments about work than behaviour and three times more negative comments about behaviour than work. You need to redress this imbalance and give at least as many positive comments for behaviour as for work. The words you use are very important but you will also need to remember the importance of non-verbal encouragement. Smiles, nods or 'thumbs up' can mean a lot and can be used to good effect.

What rewards can I use with groups?

If you want to maintain and improve the behaviour of the group you need to plan rewards which are enjoyable and motivating. Groups are essentially social in nature, it may be that a fun activity works as a reward, e.g. a joke telling session (managed!) or a sharing time about favourite music or TV. Another group reward (negotiated with the teacher) is 'music while you work' when you can play some music of their choice (probably quietly!) while they get on with an activity. You might also consider an extra five minute playtime (negotiated with the teacher). Occasionally it is rewarding to share a cake or some fruit.

Younger children love decorating biscuits with squeezy icing and sprinkles and anything edible is generally quite appealing to children. One effective strategy, suggested in the *Assertive Discipline* framework (Canter and Canter 1992), is called 'Marbles in a jar'.

Marbles in a jar This strategy works through positive peer group pressure. When you notice good behaviour either from individual pupils or from the group, you put a marble in the jar. You can tell the group you are doing this or do it without mentioning it – though they can notice you doing it. When the jar is full the group gets a reward. This can be quite effective in keeping children 'on track' especially if you can put marbles in when you notice the good behaviour of children who are normally quite difficult to manage.

Consequences of inappropriate behaviour

You need to be aware of trouble brewing and do something quickly before things get difficult. You can usually sense when the group is getting restless and you might need to consider changing something to settle them again. It is often the activity itself which needs changing.

If it is too hard or too easy then some pupils will start playing up, especially if they are bored. You need all your best acting skills to be enthusiastic and make the work interesting. You need to remember to give a warning as a first reaction:

'Andrew, this is a warning. I will have to move you away from the group if you carry on. Now look at page 3 and get on with your work.'

If that doesn't work then removal from the group for a short period (a few minutes) is often enough to act as an effective sanction:

'Andrew, I want you to sit at the table over there and get on with your work, you can rejoin the group when I can see that you are working'.

If that still doesn't work you may need to involve the teacher:

'Andrew, either get on with your work or I will have to speak to Mrs Smith about your behaviour'.

Reactive strategies

You do need a plan, however, for reacting when things really do go wrong. If you notice pupils starting to have a go at each other either verbally or physically then you need to act swiftly. A clear assertive message may do the trick, 'Stop that *now*'. You will then need to sit the pair apart and distract them from further confrontation by giving them explicit calming instructions. 'Sit there and take a deep breath' or providing an activity which is distracting.

You need to be careful if a fight starts. Stay calm and do not try to pull the fighters apart. If you touch them you might end up with a black eye yourself! If a clear 'STOP' message does not work then you will need to get the teacher involved.

Some helpful strategies

Here are some strategies which teachers find helpful and which assistants can also use, based on the work of M. E. Bernard (1995). You will find them useful in both groupwork and with individual pupils.

Ignoring of behaviour

Sometimes it is best to ignore 'low level' behaviours but you need to be aware of what to ignore, when to ignore, how to ignore and for how long. You also need to know what to do when ignoring is not working. Ignoring is best used with 'notice me' (attention-seeking) behaviours. The general principle is to firmly, decisively, ignore the pupil's misbehaviour. Act, for a short time, as if the pupil does not exist. Notice any pupils in the room who are doing as you ask and praise them. This will often prompt the pupil to behave too. You can then praise them for this on task behaviour. 'James, you've got your hand up. That's good, what's your question?' In this way the pupil doesn't get your attention (remember he's looking for attention) when he's off task, but when he is on task.

Eye messages

You can communicate a lot by looking at pupils in certain ways. Eye messages can communicate that you are annoyed, are silently questioning, or are communicating happiness or pleasure. They can be very effective!

Know when to ignore disruptive behaviour!

Facial messages

Along with our eyes, we use facial expressions to convey meaning. You will probably recognise these signals: the wry or happy smile, raised eye-brows, appreciation, the good-for-you expression, or other signs of annoyance, frustration, resolution. We regularly, combine eye messages and facial messages.

Simple direction

A simple direction should express your intent clearly and simply. It is assertive and says what you want from the pupil. It is not an involved discussion. 'Simon put that away now and finish your work.' 'Donna, don't touch the models they are not dry yet.' In using directions you need to stand close to the pupil without invading his or her body space. Use firm eye messages and be assertive, calm and clear in what you say. You may need to repeat the directions using the child's name again or just simply say the name. This is sometimes called the 'broken record' technique as you repeat yourself. Do not get diverted by the pupil!

Simple warning

A simple warning is brief, clear and decisive and should be the first step in a menu of sanctions. Let the child know you are giving a warning and do it calmly, 'Richard, if you continue to push and shove Nicola in the lunch line, you will have to go to the back.'

Rule re-statement

This reminds the child of the classroom rules, e.g. 'Stephen, you know the class rule about swearing.'

Simple questions

This is your attempt to challenge the pupil to reflect upon his/her own behaviour. It is very effective. You can use two basic questions. Look directly at the pupil and ask calmly 'What are you doing?' Most children reply 'Nothing'.

Of course they are doing something so tell them what, exactly, they are doing. Briefly, say 'You're talking loudly during maths.' 'What should you be doing?' (second question). If the child comes up with an appropriate answer give a brief eye message and move off as if he/she is going to do what he/she should be doing.

Distractions and diversions

You can often anticipate trouble and prevent misbehaviour by diverting or distracting the pupil as he or she appears to be beginning to cause a disruption. If you sense a disruption coming, invite some assistance from the pupil, ask the pupil a question, come up close to the pupil speaking quietly about their work, or invite another pupil to work with the pupil causing the disruption.

Clear choices

It is better for you to give pupils a clear choice rather than making threats you can't carry out. Use language that doesn't box you in. For example, in extreme cases of misbehaviour, you can say 'Ian you can either work by the fair rules of the group or we'll have to ask you to leave.' Not, 'I'll make you leave.' In fact, effective discipline is based on teaching pupils responsibility for their own behaviour by offering them choices. This is why you need to use questions, brief directions, give options, follow-up with negotiations later and give rational/logical consequences.

Defusion statements

Defusing a situation where a pupil is likely to misbehave means saying something 'light', 'witty' or humorous which takes the heat out of the moment. This can work really well – often the most successful teachers are good at this and you can learn a lot by watching and listening to the way they use defusion statements. But remember not to use sarcasm, which makes things worse!

Deflection comments

Rather than getting into a pupil's power-struggle and conflict with you ('I'm not going to do this and you can't make me.'), use a deflective comment such as 'I can see you're angry, we'll talk about this later.' Don't rise to the bait as this will wind things up, then give positive attention to others 'on task'.

Assertive message

In being assertive, state your feelings: the rule being broken, how the pupil's wrong actions are affecting you or others. Be sure to distinguish between the pupil and his/her wrong action. Convey anger assertively in 'I' messages...

'I am angry about your behaviour.'

'Paul, I cannot teach when you're making all that noise. You know our classroom rules.' Assertive messages state one's rights and protects the rights of the other members of the class. They can be used with a whole group of pupils, or one-on-one.

Broken record technique

This is a verbal strategy that re-asserts your direction using the same form of words repetitively 3 to 4 times. When a pupil gets argumentative or quarrelsome wanting to deflect you from the situation, you can 'block' the argument by briefly reminding the pupil of the class rules.

'Jack please go back to your seat. You know the rule.'

'But I was just getting a pencil.'

'Jack please get back to your seat. You know the rule.'

'It's not fair, your always picking on me.'

'Jack...'

Take the pupil aside

It may be useful in some situations to quietly call the pupil aside from the group (or even briefly outside the door of the class) to let him or her know that their behaviour is unacceptable. By taking the pupil aside you can minimize embarrassment. It is brief and allows the pupil to explain what he or she is doing and why he or she is behaving contrary to classroom rules. If the pupil is upset, it gives him or her a brief private right of reply. Be sure the pupil knows what he or she ought to be doing when he/she goes back in. If the pupil is very upset, let him or her cool off and settle down before resuming work.

ACTION BOX

Practise giving the step-by-step instructions for a routine you want pupils to follow.

STEP	WORDS YOU USE
1. Start with a signal	?
2. Wait for attention	?
3. Reminder not to start until you say	?
4. Say *what* you want the group to do	?
5. Explain *how* you want them to do it	?
6. Give a clear message that they can start	?
7. Praise those who get on and do it	?

Chapter 7

Managing the difficult behaviour of individual pupils: strategies that work

In almost every class there are one or two pupils whose behaviour is quite demanding – these are the ones who, when they are absent, the teacher breathes a sigh of relief! (teachers say that they rarely seem to be absent.) But teachers are concerned about such pupils because their job is to get on and teach the class, and any child who stops them doing so causes irritation, frustration and sometimes anger. Most teachers want difficult pupils to settle down and to get on with learning and certainly, those with good classroom management skills are able to deal with 99 per cent of disruptive incidents. However, teaching staff do recognise and welcome the contribution of assistants in supporting individual children who display difficult behaviour. Often teachers do not have the time they need to work with youngsters who are troubling or difficult and value the work of assistants especially if the assistant has those particular skills and qualities required to support the pupils effectively. So what are the 'particular' skills required?

In order to work positively with children and young people who pose particular challenges it is necessary to know:

- What might be causing the behaviour to occur? Some analysis of where it is coming from.
- How to think about where to start (as in Chapter 5).
- Particular strategies which can solve particular problems.

What might be causing the difficult behaviour?

Let's go back to an idea discussed earlier in this book – the need for children to 'belong' to a group and to be valued by others as part of the group whether that is in the class, the playground or the family. An American psychiatrist called Rudolf Dreikurs has contributed much in this area. He based his ideas on those of the psychologist Alfred Adler. One of Dreikurs main themes is: 'Man is a social being and his main desire is to belong' (Dreikurs and Cassel 1972). The trouble is some children have learned behaviours which do not help them to belong to the group and those behaviours frequently have the opposite effect.

You might think, 'Why do we need to know what is causing the problem? – it's the solutions we need!' Well, if we have some knowledge about where the behaviour is coming from, then that will give us clues about the strategies we need to intervene effectively – different sources of inappropriate behaviour require different management techniques.

How will I know how to respond?

You can use a technique called *emotional mirroring*. This means recognising your own emotional reaction to any presenting behaviour and using that to know how to respond. It is not helpful if we react without thinking as we may be doing exactly the wrong thing. Dreikurs and Cassel (1972) said that children try to belong to the group but some have learned inappropriate ways of doing this and they describe four patterns of behaviour which children use to get their needs met.

Attention seeking
Power seeking
Revenge seeking
Escape by withdrawal

How do I know which is which?

Pupils who are *attention seeking* are often described by teachers as follows:

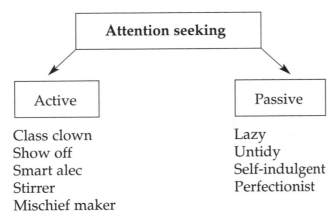

Active	Passive
Class clown	Lazy
Show off	Untidy
Smart alec	Self-indulgent
Stirrer	Perfectionist
Mischief maker	

Of course all children need attention and most get it through the teacher's approval of them conforming to class routines and working well. Some children, however, think that they have to behave in ways which cause adults to take a lot of notice of them, whether these behaviours are perceived as good or bad by the adults concerned. In general these behaviours produce irritation and annoyance on the part of the adult. These children do not cause major difficulties but rather more the low-level difficulties which can be very wearing over time.

Pupils who are *power seeking* are often described by their teachers as follows:

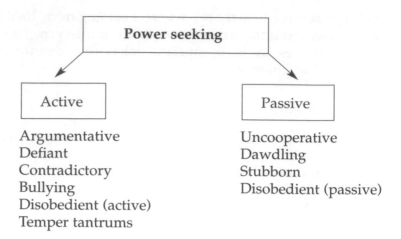

These behaviours often emerge as a stage beyond attention seeking when needs for approval have not been met. They are more difficult to manage because they challenge the authority of the adult. These behaviours often stem from insecurity and the pupils view that they can only belong to the group if they are in charge and controlling their environment. When a pupil shows these power seeking behaviours the adult on the receiving end often feels angry. 'How dare you challenge me!' is a common reaction. Such behaviours can easily rattle the adult if not handled effectively.

Pupils who are *revenge seeking* are often described by their teachers as follows:

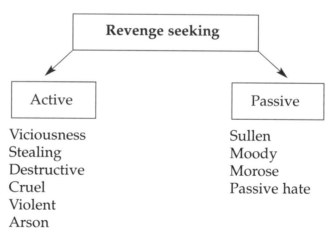

These behaviours are probably the most difficult to help. Such pupils seem deliberately to hurt others – they cause strong reactions of anger, disgust and hostility in adults, who often feel they have to retaliate. They seem to convey the message 'No one likes me, so why should I bother' from the pupil. These pupils have often been hurt themselves in some way and feel they need to get their own back on 'life, the universe and everything'. They seem to say 'I can only belong if I hurt others as much as they hurt me.'

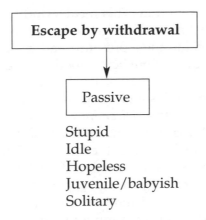

Stupid
Idle
Hopeless
Juvenile/babyish
Solitary

By definition, there are no active descriptions of *escape by withdrawal* types of behaviour! When other strategies don't work, the pupil resorts to giving up, feeling unable to cope with the demands upon them. Often these are pupils who feel they have no choices in life and no ability to change things for themselves. They make adults working with them feel like giving up, provoked by the mirrored response of helplessness.

The interesting thing is that we can use our own 'gut reactions' (see Box below) to the child's behaviour to find out what strategy the child is using, and once we know that, we have more chance of doing the right thing to manage that behaviour.

So if we feel...	...the behaviour is likely to be
Irritation, annoyance	Attention seeking
Anger, 'How dare you challenge me'	Power seeking
Hurt, disgust, 'How could anyone do that?'	Revenge seeking
Frustration, hopelessness, impatience	Escape by withdrawal

So what? If children are trying to belong to the group by using the wrong strategies, what can we do about it?

The first thing here is to DO NO HARM and that means not reacting in the way our emotions or 'gut reaction' suggests but to think before we act. If we are tempted to react to attention seeking by annoyance, power seeking by power control, revenge seeking by revenge or withdrawal by withdrawing then we will only reinforce the behaviours and make them more likely to occur again. So if the child is:

- Trying to be the centre of attention ⟶ DO NOT give negative attention.

Instead use the *positive attention* rule. It is likely that attention seeking pupils are in fact attention needing and they are going to get your attention one way or another and take your time up somehow. So it's better to get in first with positive attention before they cause you to react with negative attention. This means finding positive things to say about the child at an early stage in the day or in the activity and showing that you value their presence and their contribution. It is really important to 'catch them being good' before they can catch you catching them being bad! It may be hard to find something to say but make a real effort to do this and things will improve.

Lee Canter, in *Assertive Discipline* (Canter and Canter 1992) observes (as a joke), that for some children all you might be able to say is 'I liked the way you breathed today!' This is clearly rather extreme, but reinforces the importance of finding *something* positive. Keep watching out for ways to give positive messages. If pupils receive these messages consistently from you, their self-esteem will be raised and the need for attention will gradually diminish as they start to feel more secure about themselves.

- If the child is trying to dominate or control ⟶ DO NOT fight or confront.

If you do start a power struggle and 'win' then the pupil is the loser and will bear a grudge. If you do nothing, the pupil will 'win' and you will lose and feel negative towards the pupil.

Winning is temporary, all it does is sour the relationship and it makes the behaviour likely to occur again. What you need to look for is a 'win-win' outcome. How do you do this? When a pupil confronts you, refusing to cooperate, you must stay calm and you need to maintain some control. You can do this by giving the pupil a get out and playing for time.

'I expect you'll do this once you have thought about it. It would be really good if you can make the right choice and get on with it.'

Perhaps the pupil is refusing to do the activity and is rude to you. Rather than retaliating it is better to recognise the feelings that are being communicated. A response might be,

'Look Becky, I know you don't like French and find it hard but it has to be done before you can go out at break so let's have a go.'
Once the pupil has settled it is a better time to refer to the rudeness.

'Becky, when you were rude to me, I felt concerned and upset because I don't expect to be treated that way. Don't let it happen again, OK?'
If these strategies don't work you may need to involve the teacher.

- If the pupil is trying to devalue or destroy the group through revenge tactics ⟶ DO NOT punish.

Punishing simply serves to make the pupil seek even more revenge and the behaviour escalates. Because their actions hurt and seem deliberate, we feel justified in punishing, in 'getting even' but this leads to more revenge tactics by the pupil. A problem solving approach is more helpful.

You might work with the teacher to set up 'circle time' or group activities where the issues are raised and the pupil can learn to understand the effects of their actions on others. It is often helpful to set up a friendship group who can make positive comments about the pupil including him or her in group activities. If damage has been done, then it is appropriate for the pupil to be involved in repairing that damage. It may mean giving up time or pocket money to do so but this is a better strategy than exclusion from the group.

- If the pupil is trying to escape by withdrawal ⟶ DO NOT do it for them.

It is very tempting, when faced with a passive, lethargic pupil to do the task or activity for them but of course, this serves to reinforce their helplessness. 'She will do it for me, so why should I bother.' These pupils need to be challenged but not with huge targets which are not achievable. For pupils like this you need to focus on small steps of achievement and give plenty of encouragement. Start with work that might interest them, set targets which are quickly achieved and reward any progress. These pupils respond well to having their success shared with teachers and parents so if you can give notes or certificates and share these with the parents or carers then this will begin to reverse the downward spiral of hopelessness.

KEY POINT

Children seek to 'belong to the group'. Some just don't know how to behave in order to do this effectively. You can help them learn new skills so they can achieve this.

Planning a structured behaviour programme for an individual pupil

(This plan follows the framework described in Chapter 5.)

There are a number of points to bear in mind when planning a behaviour programme. It should be planned with the teacher for maximum effect and should be:

Workable	Makes sense to you and the pupil and has clear targets. It will work best if all adults who work with the pupil are clear about the plan (teachers, parents, assistants).
Achievable	You should plan it so that the pupil is successful.
Realistic	Don't try to change all 'bad' behaviour at once. Start with one thing and work in steps towards success. It should be the right thing for the pupil in the situation, e.g. choosing 'staying in seat' when other children are moving around is not realistic.
Manageable	It should be easy for you to monitor and record results.

Step one

Write a short list of those behaviours you want to reduce. Next to these behaviours write the ones you want to see instead, e.g.

Unwanted behaviours	Desired behaviours
Shouting out	Listening/working quietly
Getting out of seat	Staying in seat

Step two

Do an observation of the child. Become a 'fly on the wall' for half an hour and watch what is going on. Make a chart so that you can record what is happening. This will give you baseline information and provide a starting point. Here is an example of an observation chart:

OBSERVATION SHEET

Name:_____

Lesson:_____ Time of day:_____

Time	Shouts out	Out of seat	'On task'
10.00–10.05	3	2	3 mins
10.05–10.10	2	0	2 mins
10.10–10.15	2	1	1 min
10.15–10.20	0	0	0 mins
10.20–10.25	0	1	4 mins
10.25–10.30	2	2	2 mins
TOTAL	9	6	12/30

From this observation it would make sense to target shouting out as a priority. You may want to share these results with the pupil to agree you are aiming for a zero score but in the first week it might be more realistic to go for e.g. six – whatever reduction seems realistic and actionable. You would then explain to the pupil that the behaviour you want is 'keeping quiet in lesson time and raise hand to speak'.

Step three

Review your list in step one. You may have noticed other behaviours which become priorities. Decide which particular behaviour you want to encourage, e.g. staying in seat, keeping hands to self, staying quiet and putting hand up to say something.

Step four: environment analysis

Now look at what you might do to prevent this behaviour occurring in the first place. Consider whether you can change the location, peer group, subject, activity in order to eliminate or reduce the unwanted behaviour. For example:

If a pupil always gets into trouble when seated next to another particular pupil then don't allow them to sit together.

If a pupil starts distracting others shortly after a task has begun, ensure the task is clear and achievable when it is given.

If a pupil finds it hard to get started on a task, ensure he/she has all equipment necessary before you start.

Can any of the following be changed to prevent the behaviour happening in the first place?

Can these be changed?	YES	NO	HOW? and WHO?
Location of pupil e.g. proximity to teacher			
Location of pupil (sitting beside whom?)			
Subject lesson			
Task			
Assistant			
Teacher (e.g. parallel groups)			
Child's physical state			
Child's emotional state			

Step five: teach new skills

Children need to learn how to behave. You may need to demonstrate appropriate behaviour by role play or by pointing out others modelling the right behaviour. The child may need considerable practice. Role reversal where you play the part of the child, and the child the teacher can increase perception. For example:

'This is how I want you to come into the classroom' (demonstrate).

'I want you to keep your hands together on the table when I'm speaking' (demonstrate).

'I like the way John has started work straight away. I want you to do that.'

'I want you to keep quiet when I'm talking and put your hand up when you want to say something.'

Step six

Share the results of your observation with the pupil. Explain that you are going to work together to encourage, e.g. 'staying in seat' by cutting down the times he or she is out of his or her seat. Ask the pupil what needs to happen in order for them to stay in their seat. Involve the pupil in setting a target for the next similar lesson, i.e. cut down from 8 times to 4 times out of seat. Monitor and check how things are going, 'How's it going?' 'You're doing well.' 'You're remembering to sit in your seat. Well done.'

Problem behaviour	Target behaviour (positively phrased)
Shouting out.	Keep quiet and raise hand to speak.
Out of seat.	Stay in seat.
Distracting others by poking.	Keep hands, feet and objects to yourself.
Seeking a great deal of adult attention.	Work alone for five minutes.

Step seven: positive reinforcement of appropriate behaviour

It is really important to 'catch children being good' and notice that behaviour by giving a positive verbal or non-verbal message. If you want to change behaviour rather than just control it, then you will need to learn the skills of reinforcement. Give praise when the child conforms to normally expected standards of behaviour in school.

Positive messages can be related to behaviour as well as work and it is good to let children know why you are pleased, e.g. 'Jenny, I like the way you came into the classroom this morning.' 'Jason, you listened carefully all through that explanation. Well done.'

I like the way you are sitting quietly

Rewards, or positive consequences of good behaviour, are very important. They show the child that he or she is succeeding and it is worthwhile to succeed. These are given when targets are met. But for rewards to be motivating, they have to mean something to the child so your first job is to find out what is a real reward for the child. Negotiate a reward for meeting the target (make the target easy to achieve). Ask the pupil what he or she would like as a reward. Suggest one if he or she doesn't come up with anything realistic. Suggestions for rewards would be:

Infant/Junior
Bubble blowing.
Decorating plain biscuits with icing and sprinkles.
Extra time on the computer.
A favourite game.
Music while you work.
Certificate to take home to parents.
Special responsibility.

Secondary
Extra computer time.
Pen.
Keyring.
Certificate to take home.
Cooking.
Special responsibility.
Free ticket to school disco.

The lottery principle

It is sometimes even more motivating if several rewards are possible, each written on a card and put in an envelope. One 'reward' should be extra special. The pupil takes a chance on choosing a reward and might get the star prize.

Step eight

If the target is achieved give reward and praise and record on a chart for the pupil to see. Set a new target for next similar lesson, e.g. twice out of seat.

If the target is not achieved, make it easier and say 'We'll try again tomorrow.'

Step nine

Continue for two weeks giving the negotiated reward for targets which are achieved. Review the programme. Continue to make targets clear and to teach any new behavioural skills the child needs and review environmental factors.

Step ten

Do another observation and compare it with the original. Use the same lesson and same time of day. Is there any improvement? If not, why not? Consider appropriateness of task, peer group and environment.

Step eleven

Choose another behaviour, e.g. 'Now that you're able to stay in your seat most of the time, we're going to choose another target. What do you think we could work on next?'

Remember to keep a written or picture record of what is achieved. The pupil might enjoy doing this themselves, e.g. putting stickers on a chart. Negotiate a 'super reward' for the pupil after two weeks of improvement. Send any good news home to share with parents.

Ensure the task the pupil is given is at the right level for his or her ability. Problems often occur when pupils are bored or the task is too hard.

Step twelve

If you have provided an optimum environment for the pupil, e.g. task at right level, sitting by non-troublemakers, etc. and the pupil deliberately chooses not to follow an instruction then you will need to discuss with the teacher what sanction to apply. The first sanction should be a warning, e.g. 'If you keep on getting up out of your seat,

Sometimes you just *have* to respond

you will be moved away from the group.' Children dislike being moved to sit away from their friends so this is quite an effective 'mild' sanction. This should only be done for short periods at a time.

Evidence suggests that it is not the severity of the sanction but the consistency with which it is applied that makes the difference.

What if things go badly wrong?

Reactive strategies

This is unlikely to happen but there are some incidents which are too disruptive to be ignored and you have to react quickly, e.g. if a fight breaks out. You might sometimes need to use physical restraint to stop things getting worse and as an assistant, you need to discuss with the class teacher, SENCO or head of year whether you have permission and know how to restrain pupils physically (see p. 103). This is not normally part of your role.

Repairing damaged relationships

When things have gone wrong, there are usually hurt feelings on all sides. It is important that you, as the adult, take steps to heal the rift. Sometimes it will be appropriate for you to help the pupil to make amends for the trouble caused. This may be through an apology or some 'social service' in school. In rebuilding damaged relationships it will be helpful to discuss what caused the problem situation and make plans with the pupil to avoid it happening again. Try to start each day as a new day and expect that things will improve. It will be helpful if parents can be involved in this planning, but normally it will be the teacher who liaises with parents.

Sometimes, in the course of your work you will come across children or young people who seem particularly troubled, unhappy, depressed or anxious, as a result of particular circumstances in their life. Most pupils have patches when they feel low particularly during adolescence and particularly following the breakdown of relationships, e.g. parental divorce, family breakdown, family bereavement or boy/girl problems. Most pupils get over these traumas but sometimes, if the family breakdown goes on or if circumstances are particularly difficult they can have long-term adverse effects, often in the form of mental health problems. You will not be expected, as part of your job, to provide in-depth counselling as that is something which needs to be delivered by a trained counsellor but you can learn the skills of active listening which can really help the pupils you work with in managing their emotions. If difficulties persist however and you become concerned about the pupil, e.g. if he or she talks about suicide then you certainly need to alert the teacher and the head teacher. If you are going to work one-to-one with pupils it is important that you follow these guidelines for your own safety and that of the pupil. (It is extremely unlikely that you will be accused of anything or be attacked by the pupil but you need to be safe.)

Working one-to-one with troubled children or young people

- Have the permission of the teacher and the parent to do this and let them know where and when.
- Use a room which has a window and you can be seen from the outside by anyone passing.
- Keep the door slightly ajar and take the seat nearer to the door.
- If the pupil asks you to keep secrets, explain that you can to a certain degree but there are some things which you *have* to share, i.e. if you feel the child is in danger or endangering someone else, these being if the pupil is being abused, or abusing, physically, sexually or emotionally. The Child Protection guidelines in your school will give details.

Active listening is a way of working with pupils which enables them to express their feelings and to think about ways forward. You can learn and practise the skills which active listening requires.

What is active listening?

What are the skills I need for active listening?

You need to develop certain verbal and non-verbal skills to be a good active listener but before you can start you need both the right mind-set and the right setting for it to be effective.

Setting   It is no use trying to grab a few minutes with a pupil on the school corridor or in between lessons. There will just not be enough time and probably too many other distractions. Ideally, you need a comfortable room – soft seating and no distractions. You need to have cleared a slot of at least 15 minutes with the teacher and with the pupil and be prepared to insist that you are not disturbed.

You will find that sitting at a 45 degree angle to the child is better than directly opposite as this is less confrontational.

Attitude   You will not be able to do this effectively if you are in a state yourself! In order to be a good active listener you need to suspend your own anxieties and fears and be prepared to concentrate on the pupil for the time you spend with them.

Try to show empathy – that is a real desire to understand things from the pupil's point of view. Communicating your interest is also very important, the pupil needs to feel that you are genuinely concerned on their behalf and feel positive towards them. Showing an interest in their interests and using language which is clear and understandable also helps communication.

Non-verbal behaviour   You can communicate a lot to others by your non-verbal behaviour, in fact in many situations non-verbal behaviour communicates more than the words you use. For example, imagine that your partner comes home later than arranged having been to the pub and you had cooked a really nice meal. You could smile and say in a soothing voice, 'That's OK, I don't mind, go to the pub anytime.' However, were you to say these same words but stand up with your arms folded, foot tapping on the floor, no smiling and using a 'fed-up' voice, your non-verbal language and tone of voice would be much more powerful than the words you use. So do be aware of the power of non-verbal communication. When there is a discrepancy between the words we use and our body language, it is the body language that is 'heard'.

Try to remember the following ideas about non-verbal behaviour when you work with pupils:

- Use 'open' gestures – this means sitting in a relaxed pose without folding your arms or crossing your legs as these are 'closed' gestures.
- Appropriate eye contact – do look at the pupil even if they are not looking at you, this demonstrates commitment.
- Nodding – when the child or young person talks to you nodding communicates positive regard and listening.
- Smiling – don't forget to smile as a welcome and during your time together although you will need to look serious and concerned if serious issues are raised.

Verbal communication

Use of the right words and phrases is very important in getting active listening right. You will probably need to learn certain phrases or 'lead in' sentences which will make it easier for the pupil to respond to you.

Brenda Mallon, in her book *An Introduction to Counselling Skills for Special Educational Needs* (1987) provides a useful framework for active listening as follows:

Active listening skills

Types	Purpose	Examples
1. Warmth, support	To help the pupil to feel at ease	I'd like to help... Are you able to tell me about your concern?
2. Clarification	To get the complete 'story' from the pupil To assist the pupil in exploring the whole issue	Can you tell me more about it? Do you mean...?
3. Restatement	To check our meaning is the same as the pupil's To show understanding	From what you are saying I understand that... So, you've decided to...
4. Encouragement	To encourage the pupil	I realise this is difficult for you, but you're doing really well...
5. Reflective	To act as a mirror for the pupil to see what is being communicated To help pupils evaluate their feelings behind the words	You feel that... It was very hard for you to accept... You felt angry and upset when they...
6. Summarising	To bring together the areas discussed so far To provide a starting point for future work	These are the main points which have emerged... As I see it, your main concern seems to be...

It is really effective to follow these steps, starting from an acknowledgement of how the pupil is feeling. 'John, I can see you are feeling upset, are you able to talk about what has upset you?' Once you have clarified what the issues are, and used the framework above to guide your conversation, you will reach a point at which the pupil thinks that you understand what the problem is. It is vital that you reach a point at which you can relate the pupil's concern, check it out with him or her and he or she says 'Yes that's right'. Only then can you move on effectively to consider possible solutions to the problem.

Problem solving

The following ideas can be helpful in problem solving:

- Share the problem, 'What can we think of to improve things for you?'
- Look for times when the problem isn't there, e.g. 'Are there any times when Becky isn't calling you names?'
- Suggest changes in the patterns which lead to the problem (place, time, language, particular lessons, etc.).
- Are there times in the past when the pupil has overcome the problem. How did they do it?
- Search for examples which show the pupil to be capable, a good friend, a good 'avoider' of difficult situations, etc. This helps the pupil to view themselves as resourceful.
- Use the videotape analogy – pupils relate well to this analogy (most being frequent users of videotapes!).

Imagine your life is being recorded on video. If you could rewind and tape over some bits which bits would they be? What would you be doing instead? What would be happening around you? How could you have done things differently? Now fast forward (to a day, a week, a month, whatever is appropriate). What would you like to see yourself doing on the video? Who would be around? Where would you be? How can you make this happen? Who can help you to make it happen? What would they be doing?

It is often helpful to arrange to see the pupil again – weekly sessions can be used – in order to help in keeping them 'on track'. It is also important to have boundaries to these sessions – to be clear about beginnings, endings and how long the sessions are.

As an assistant you may not be required to work in such depth with pupils but there are certainly some assistants, mainly in secondary schools, or in schools for pupils with emotional and behavioural difficulties, who work with quite troubled pupils. Whatever your involvement, you will find that active listening skills help you to communicate with pupils whose behaviour is difficult to manage.

ACTION BOX

Think of examples of difficult behaviour you have experienced. Work out from your emotional reaction, what needs the child is seeking to meet (attention seeking, power seeking, revenge seeking, escape by withdrawal).

Behaviour	My emotional reaction	Child's needs

Chapter 8

Teaching good behaviour and new skills

As described in Chapter 5, good behaviour can be taught (see 'teaching new skills'). Behaviour is learned, and can be 'unlearned' if 'good' behaviours are substituted for 'bad'. It is important to hold on to the fact that behaviour *can* change although on a bad day it sometimes seems hard to imagine this! So what particular behaviours and skills might we want to teach the children we work with? We discussed earlier in the book how rules and routines can be learned. As an assistant you will be working to help the pupil conform to normally expected standards of behaviour in the classroom. What is meant by 'normally expected' can vary from teacher to teacher but in most cases it means that the pupil comes into school with a good attitude, follows the directions of the teacher and generally does not cause any serious disruption. Of course all children misbehave from time to time and may have to be redirected from talking or socialising when they should be working. But it can be quite a challenge to change some of the more persistent behaviours which cause problems especially in adolescence.

Understanding emotions – your own and others

We have seen how understanding our own emotions can help in understanding the emotions of the pupil. There are some ways of working which can help you in helping pupils to manage their own emotions in ways which will make things better for them. In order to do this the pupil will need to develop empathy, that is an understanding of how another person is feeling and thinking. The ability to attribute feelings and emotions to others cannot develop until a child has a basic understanding of their own emotions. One of the most powerful ways of doing this is to use role play, asking the pupil to play the part of different characters in an event or story then getting them to describe their feelings.

For younger children, it can be helpful to act out fairy tales, e.g. *Cinderella* or *The Billy Goats Gruff*. These stories have themes of fairness, unfairness, bullying and victimisation which can be helpful in developing emotional understanding. Older pupils also respond well to role play situations, either fictional or real. Sometimes it can help to act out a real life situation in which conflict has occurred, and analyse the emotions and reactions of each player.

Another technique which is useful is 'Pressing the right buttons'. I often use this analogy with children and young people when I am asked to work with them because of their concern about behaviour. As it is something they can visualise and is within their experience, they often respond well. Essentially it is about pressing the right buttons to get the drink they want from a drinks machine.

> *'Imagine we have a drinks machine here and it has Coca-cola, Lilt and Fanta, which one would you want?* (Wait for response – imagine it is Lilt). *Okay so if you want a can of Lilt what do you have to do to get the Lilt?* (Wait for response – typically – put money into the machine and press the button.) *What would happen if you pressed the button for Coca-cola?* (Wait for response.) *Is that what you wanted?* (No.) *So to be sure you want Lilt you have to press the right button for Lilt. Now teachers are like that – imagine they are a drinks machine. What do* you *want?* (Prompt – that they want to get through the lesson without a bad outcome for them – detention or whatever.) *You need to put something in – some effort. And what do you need to do to press the right 'buttons' on the teacher?* (Prompt – smile, look ready for work, keep quiet, don't start trouble, etc.) *Then you might get what you want.'*

This analogy helps pupils to think of alternative ways of responding to meet both the needs of the teacher and their own needs and can help them understand their own feelings and those of the teacher.

Developing play skills

The different stages of play help to prepare a child for their interactions with the world and in particular, help them to understand the differences between people. This play is an important foundation for the development of relationships with other people and for developing social skills.

Many children with more complex emotional or behavioural difficulties may have missed out on early play experiences so, as an assistant, your role might be to help them learn to play in a creative and constructive way. You can do this by observing the child playing and then guiding, rather than leading, the course of play. Once the child cooperates with you in play then you can involve other children in cooperative (and fun!) play situations, reinforcing appropriate social interactions.

Anger management

One common problem which some children and young people have is anger management. There are a considerable number of pupils who seem to be 'on a short fuse' or highly volatile and who are easily roused to anger. This may stem from poor self-esteem or frustration or home role models. Whatever the source, it results in problems for children at school. Lack of self-control can lead children and young people into situations which they cannot pull back from and later regret. This is why it is important to teach such children how to recognise their angry feelings and how to manage those feelings so that they do not get into trouble. Some teachers are trained to run anger management groups and you may have a support role in these groups which aim to help children redirect their anger in positive ways. Pupils who learn to manage their anger in positive and socially acceptable ways are more likely to develop lasting peer and adult relationships and generally do better in school.

How can I support pupils who get angry?

You can give support by helping the pupils you work with understand
the following ideas: (from O'Rourke and Worzbyt 1996).

1. The use of violent or aggressive behaviour as an expression of anger is unacceptable. Fighting, hitting, and hurtful words are not OK even when you are angry.
2. All feelings are OK. How you express your feelings is what matters.
3. Children can become angry when they are teased, called names, not allowed to play with others, when things do not go the right way for them, and when their feelings are hurt by others. Help children to talk about things, situations, events, and people that cause them to become angry.
4. When children become angry, they experience different signs of anger on the inside and the outside. Children may tense their muscles, get red in the face, have a knot in their stomach, get sweaty palms, talk loudly, feel like crying, and have angry and hurtful thoughts toward others. Ask children to describe the signs of anger that they experience.
5. When children become angry, they handle their anger in different ways. Children may pretend not to be angry, blame others for their anger, withdraw from the anger-producing situation, explode, and solve their problems by brainstorming helpful and responsible ideas that they can try. Help children to discuss how they handle their angry feelings.
6. Solutions to angry situations can be helpful or hurtful. Discuss with children the differences between helpful and hurtful responses to anger.
7. Children who have the most success in handling their anger in positive and responsible ways are those that have a plan for doing so. What follows is an anger management plan that you can use with the pupils you work with. This plan will help children learn what they can do about angry feelings. The steps are as follows:

Step 1: **How am I feeling right now?** What bodily signs are you experiencing that help you know that your are angry?

Step 2: **Calm down.** Before the feelings become too strong and over-powering, help children reduce their anger by taking deep breaths; thinking pleasant thoughts; and telling themselves to calm down – 'I'm OK, things will get better, etc.'

Step 3: **Problem solve.**

STOP What is my problem? Ask the child to describe their problem – what has happened?

THINK What are my choices? (Help children make a list of all the things that they could do.) After making the list, consider each solution separately by asking 'Will this solution help or hurt me, others, or property?' 'What evidence do I have that tells me this is the right thing to do?' 'What are the consequences?' 'What are the good things and bad things that could happen to me or others if I pick this solution?'

GO Go with a solution that is helpful, safe, supported by facts, and is likely to have positive consequences.

Step 4: **Evaluate.** After you have acted on your choice, think about what happened. What did you do? How did you feel? Did it work? Was it the right thing to do (helpful vs. hurtful)? What might you have done differently? Are you satisfied with how you handled your anger?

You can be a positive role model for the children you work with by demonstrating positive and acceptable methods in expressing your own anger. Likewise you can catch your children modelling appropriate methods of anger management and positively reinforce them for their actions.

Let children know that hitting, biting, screaming, and temper tantrums are unacceptable expressions of anger. Tell them that there are positive things that they can do to help them get rid of their uncomfortable feelings such as punching a pillow, going outside and running around, and using the anger management four step plan above.

You will need to discuss your approaches with the class teacher. It may be that if the difficulties are excessive or persistent there may be a need for more specialist help. There are a number of helpful resources which can aid teachers and assistants in anger management work:

Anger Management: A practical guide, Faupel *et al.* (1998); *Support Groups for Children*, O'Rourke and Worzbyt (1996); *Anger Management: A six session course*, Poole Educational Psychology Service (2001).

Social skills

Quite a number of pupils have behaviour which is difficult to manage as a result of poor social skills. Social skills are socially acceptable behaviours that enable us to interact appropriately and responsibly with others in any given situation, and this includes the skills of friendship. Children who possess good social skills and know how and when to use them are successful in developing satisfying relationships with others while attaining their personal goals.

What can I do to help children learn social skills?

As an assistant you can play an important part in teaching children appropriate social skills which will make a real difference in their relationships with others and result in improved self-esteem and belonging to the group. Here are some ideas for giving support (taken from O'Rourke and Worzbyt 1996):

---

1. There are many social skills that children should learn. You first must identify what social skills the child already possesses. Then decide what skills he or she still needs that will enhance his or her relationships with others.
2. Here are a few important social skills that will benefit most children

   - To gain attention from others in appropriate ways
   - To ask others for help
   - To greet others
   - To introduce oneself to others
   - To help others
   - To speak one at a time
   - To follow home and school rules
   - To share

   - To take turns
   - To return things to their rightful place
   - To compliment others
   - To ask others to play
   - To distinguish one's own property from others
   - Tell the truth and to accept the consequences
   - To tell right from wrong
   - To say 'thank you', 'please' and 'may I?'
   - To eat with good manners

3. Observe other people and children. What behaviours do they use that please teachers and other children? Make a list of these behaviours and select those that you would like to teach the child.
4. Identify problem behaviours in the child. Help the child discard these behaviours and substitute them with more responsible social skills.

Problem	*Social skills*
The child interrupts others	Teach the child to wait for pauses in a conversation before speaking
The child does not play games according to the rules	Teach the child how to play games according to the rules
The child always finds fault with himself or herself	Teach the child how to identify positive self-behaviours and to self-affirm those positive qualities.

Teach the child new social skills using the following steps:

Step 1   Identify the social skill you would like to teach.

Step 2   Explain to the child the purpose or the benefits that he or she will gain from learning this skill. You also may want to discuss the pitfalls that children may incur if they do not learn it. The child needs to recognise the value of this social skill.

You can use videotapes, stories, and live examples of children using this social skill to help motivate the child in wanting to learn this new behaviour.

Step 3   Identify the skill components and steps (chain of behaviours) you need to teach the child to learn this social skill. One good way of identifying these steps is to observe what others do who have learned the social skill. For example, making friends is a complex social skill. What behaviours would a person display who has developed this skill? Brainstorm a list of these behaviours.

Step 4   After identifying the skill components, place them in the order of their occurrence.

Step 5   Model the behaviour. The child needs to see the social skill in action. Go through each step and explain the step as you perform it. You can either model the social skill yourself or use stories, video, or live models that can demonstrate the social skill for you. You must go slowly, provide clear and detailed directions, provide repetition in demonstrating the skill, and use a variety of different models to teach the skills.

Step 6   Help the child rehearse each step as it is being taught. He or she can be taught to verbalise out loud what he or she is doing. You also can ask the child to mentally picture himself or herself going through the steps before actually doing it.

Step 7   Provide feedback. As each step is performed, let the child know how he or she is doing. Be very clear in giving the feedback. Let the child know what he or she is doing correctly and guide him or her in shaping each step.

Step 8   Help the child practise the steps in sequence. Provide positive feedback and lots of praise for doing it well.

Step 9   Once the child learns a new social skill, help him or her identify all the different places and ways in which it can be used.

Step 10 Give the child a 'homework' practice assignment. Have him or her use the new social skill in another setting. Discuss with the child how things went. Help the child continue to improve upon his or her ability to use the social skill.

About bullying

Bullying is a subject which arouses strong feelings. Most of us can remember times from our own schooldays when we were unfairly treated either by teachers or by other children and some of these experiences can be quite destructive. Bullying is a particularly negative experience and should be prevented as far as possible in schools. All schools should have an anti-bullying policy and you should read it so that you know school procedures.

What is bullying?

You will get many children coming to you complaining of being bullied but what they are usually talking about is a single incident. Bullying is when the child is persistently targeted by another child or group. A definition is a follows:

> Bullying is behaviour which can be defined as the repeated attack, physical, psychological, social or verbal, by those in a position of power, which is formally or situationally defined, on those who are powerless to resist, with the intention of causing distress for their own gain or gratification.
>
> (Besag 1989)

If you are aware that bullying is going on, then you need to alert the class teacher and provide evidence of what you have observed. It is very tempting to 'jump in with both feet' and punish the bully but this often serves to make things worse and does not lead to a 'best for both' outcome. Your role may be in helping the 'victim' to learn better social skills for handling the bullying behaviour or to help the child who bullies to understand the effect of their behaviour on others. The methods which help children understand the bad feelings generated by bullying seem to work best in preventing further incidents. Lucky Duck Publications have produced a number of really helpful videos and booklets about how to prevent and manage bullying incidents.

KEY POINT

Start each day as a new day. Have positive expectations that the child will improve.

Chapter 9

Attention Deficit/ Hyperactivity Disorder (AD/HD)

In your work as an assistant it is very likely that you will work with some children who have particular behaviour difficulties which stem from physiological or medical causes rather than social causes, i.e. they are mainly to do with nature rather than nurture. The majority of difficulties under the heading of emotional and behavioural difficulties (EBD), stem from causes which are more to do with nurture, environment and upbringing. Attention Deficit/ Hyperactivity Disorder (AD/HD), Asperger's Syndrome and autism are three labels given to children whose behaviour is sometimes difficult to manage as a result of physiological or medical reasons.

What is AD/HD?

AD/HD is a term used to describe children, young people and adults who have the following characteristics:

- Impulsive behaviour and poor self-control.
- Difficulty in sustaining attention.
- Hyperactivity: the apparent need to be 'on the go' all the time.

Research suggests that about 1 in every 100 children can be described as AD/HD and that boys outnumber girls by 5 to 1. It is estimated that about 40 per cent of children who are described as having emotional and behavioural difficulties have AD/HD. There is a form of this particular difficulty called Attention Deficit Disorder (ADD) and it applies to a group of children who show the impulsivity and distractibility but not the hyperactive behaviour.

There are some factors in AD/HD which distinguish it from other emotional and behavioural difficulties:

- It is thought to have a biological basis, possibly caused by particular brain function.
- It is likely to be a lifelong condition.
- It is often improved by medication.

There has been considerable research into what causes AD/HD and there is a view from some that it is 'the medicalisation of social difficulties'. Certainly, we can all think of some children, born into 'normal' nurturing families where the children are generally settled but where there might be one child who is different from the others in that they are much more demanding and harder to manage than the others, showing the characteristics of AD/HD. These cases suggest a biological cause. There are other children who seem to develop AD/HD in reaction to major trauma or life events. Some recent American research suggests that if a child is subjected to significant physical, sexual or emotional abuse then sometimes there can be changes in brain chemistry which means that the child's arousal levels are raised. This results in Attention Deficit/ Hyperactivity Disorder. There seems to be a kind of 'frightened rabbit' effect in that the child cannot settle and seems to be on the lookout for threats much of the time. It is as if damaging experiences have caused this inability to settle and concentrate. Whatever the cause, these youngsters cause headaches for both parents and school staff because of their demanding and distractible behaviour.

AD/HD is a medical diagnosis and the drug Ritalin is often prescribed in order to help the child to concentrate and so to help him or her to settle to learn in school. As part of your work as an assistant one of your jobs might be to monitor the behaviour of the child who is taking Ritalin, working with the teacher and the school nurse.

Many adults who work with children are uncomfortable about controlling the behaviour of children using drugs, as there may be side effects – loss of appetite and sleeplessness are sometimes observed in children taking Ritalin. It can also encourage a drug dependency culture. But there are undoubtedly some children for whom it works well and they are able to become more settled in both learning and behaviour.

How will I recognise a pupil with AD/HD?

Very easily is the answer! These are often the children who stand out clearly when observing a class group. You will notice some or all of the following behaviour:

- finds difficulty in following instructions;
- acts impulsively without thinking about the consequences;
- easily distracted and forgetful;
- often doesn't listen when spoken to;
- fidgets, is restless, can't sit still;
- interferes with other children's work;
- can't stop talking, interrupts others;
- runs about when inappropriate;
- blurts out answers without waiting to be asked;
- difficulty in waiting or taking turns;
- acting impulsively without thinking about the consequences.

Although most children will demonstrate some of these behaviours some of the time, those who have several of these problems consistently and regularly are likely to have AD/HD. These children often find it hard to learn; research from the USA suggests that 90 per cent of children with AD/HD underachieve at school and 20 per cent have reading difficulties. Also, for AD/HD to be used as a description, the child must show these behaviours both at home and at school.

What can I do to support the pupil with AD/HD?

These children are often the ones who try the patience of adults to the limit. The first and most important thing you can do is to keep calm and not to let any exasperation show! Easier said than done and very difficult for parents who may need support themselves. It is very important that you do not lose your temper as this will only serve to make things worse. Another important fact to remember is that children with attention problems are more forgetful than most and are likely to turn up without equipment or homework. This usually prompts such response from adults as:

'You'd forget your head if it wasn't screwed on.'

'If I've told you once, I've told you a thousand times.'

'How many times do I have to tell you to bring your...to the lesson?'

These responses only serve as 'put downs' for the pupil and are not helpful. Try to think of practical ways to remind the pupil what they need.

Another key point to remember is that children and young people described as AD/HD live in the 'here and now' and have little thought for the future. It is therefore important to give IMMEDIATE feedback for behaviour. Positive feedback, praise, a smile or a pat on the back rewards the child for doing something well. If you can train yourself to give positive feedback frequently and consistently then you will be making a real difference. Make sure you say SPECIFICALLY what has been done right. 'Well done James, you are sitting quietly on the mat', 'Gemma, you are drawing that dog very carefully, good girl.'

It is also important to give immediate feedback for poor behaviours, this is something which is particular to the management of children with AD/HD. Again you need to be specific, 'Jack, stop hitting Daniel. It hurts him when you do that', 'Hannah, pick that litter up. We don't throw litter away in our school.'

Remember to stay calm but be firm and clear in your instructions. The pupil will not remember if you get into lengthy telling off.

The following list (Hampshire County Council 1996) gives good ideas for working with children described as having AD/HD.

(**N.B.** Many of these strategies are useful for all children who have behavioural difficulties. The ones marked * are particularly important for children with AD/HD.)

Strategies to address specific behavioural issues

1. Inattention

- *Provide frequent, immediate and consistent feedback on behaviour and redirection back to task.
- Seat pupil in a quiet area.
- Seat pupil near a good role model.
- Increase distance between desks.
- *Seat pupil away from distracting stimuli.
- Give assignments one at a time.
- Gear assignments to attention span.

- Break long assignments into smaller parts.
- Include a variety of activities during each lesson.
- Assist pupil in setting short-term goals.
- Restrict homework to that which is essential.
- Give clear, concise instructions.
- Provide written outline of lesson.
- *Cue pupil to stay on task, e.g. using a private signal.
- Let pupil share recently learned concepts, etc. with a peer still having difficulty with them.
- Pay careful attention to design of worksheets and tests.
- Use large type and provide only one or two activities per page.
- *Keep page format simple.
- *Avoid extraneous pictures or visual distracters that are not specifically and directly related to the task.
- Have white space on each page.
- Use dark black print and avoid hand-written worksheets or tests if possible.
- Write clear, simple directions.
- *Provide alternative environments with fewer distractions for taking tests.
- Allow pupil to use a tape recorder sometimes rather than always requiring written work.
- Shorten assignments. If the pupil can demonstrate adequate skill mastery in 10 or 20 questions, don't require completion of 30–40 items.

2. Excessive motor activity

- Choose the AD/HD pupil to be the one who writes keywords or ideas on the board, etc.
- *Allow opportunities for pupil to move around the room.
- Provide short break between assignments.
- Remind pupil to check work if performance is rushed or careless.
- *Plan ahead for transitions, establish rules and supervise closely.

3. Poor organisation and planning

- Establish a daily classroom routine and schedule.
- Organise desks and folders daily. Check for neatness.
- Persuade parents to use organiser trays at home marked with the day of the week so that books and work required at school that day are all together.
- A personal visual timetable may be helpful in view of the difficulty with time concepts.
- *Fasten a checklist to the pupil's desk, or put one in each subject folder/exercise book to outline the steps to be taken in following directions or checking to ensure that a task is correctly completed.
- Give notes to the pupil about key elements in the lesson.
- Use individual homework assignment charts that can go home to be signed daily by parents.

- Provide rules for getting organised.
- *Give assignments one at a time.
- Supervise recording of homework assignments.
- Check homework daily.
- Assist pupil in short-term goals in completing assignments.

4. Impulsiveness

- Keep classroom rules clear and simple.
- Ignore minor inappropriate behaviour.
- *Increase immediate rewards and consequences.
- Use careful reprimands for misbehaviour (criticise the behaviour not the child).
- Attend to positive behaviour with compliments.
- Seat pupil near a good role model or near teacher.
- Encourage the pupil to verbalise what must be done; aloud to the teacher in a one-to-one setting at first, then whispering quietly to self and finally saying silently to self.
- *Teach verbal mediation skills to reduce impulsive behaviour by modelling. Practise a structured routine of stop/listen, look/think, answer/do.

5. Non-compliance

- Praise compliant behaviour.
- *Provide immediate feedback about acceptable and unacceptable behaviour.
- Use teacher attention to reinforce positive behaviour.

6. Difficulties with peers

- *Praise appropriate social behaviour.
- Organise social skills training to teach concepts of communication, participation and cooperation.
- Define social behaviour goals with pupil and implement a reward programme.
- Encourage cooperative learning tasks with other pupils.
- Praise pupil frequently to increase esteem within the classroom.
- Assign special responsibilities to pupil in presence of peer group so others observe pupil in a positive light.

7. Poor self-esteem

- Provide reassurance and encouragement.
- Frequently compliment positive behaviour.
- *Focus on pupil's talents and accomplishments.
- Reinforce frequently when signs of frustration are noticed.

KEY POINT

Give the pupil positive messages, both verbal and non-verbal, every day.

Chapter 10

Autism and Asperger's Syndrome

If you work in a special school, it is very likely that you will come across children with autism or Asperger's Syndrome. However, more children with these disabilities are now being educated in mainstream schools and it is important that you are aware of the particular needs of this group of children and have some idea of how to manage their behaviour.

What is autism? Autism was first identified in 1943 by Leo Kanner who worked in America. He noted particularly that these children seemed to have a real difficulty in relating to other people. The characteristics originally identified by Kanner have since been modified to provide the key features of autism. These include:

- *An 'autistic' aloneness*
  This refers to an autistic child's lack of normal interaction with the world around them, and apparent lack of seeking to develop relationships with people, or even to acknowledge other people, other than as objects.
- *A desire for sameness*
  An autistic child's behaviour is often primarily aimed at keeping everything the same. They usually respond with extreme distress to even minor changes to their environment or routine. Obsessive behaviours can develop. These are felt to serve a therapeutic purpose for the child, and an increase in frequency or intensity of obsessive behaviours is a sign of increased stress.
- *A limitation in the variety of spontaneous activity*
  Linked to the desire for sameness, this exhibits itself in repetitive, monotonous behaviours. A child may seek to impose elaborate routines on their environment, which serve no logical purpose. Children with autism do not explore their world through play, but instead prefer to line up or sort toys, imposing order and structure.
- *Over-sensitivity to stimuli*
  Many children with autism are unusually sensitive to particular stimuli, including sounds, visual stimuli, smell or taste, as well as touch. A child may be sensitive to a particular pitch of sound, a shape or colour. Sensitivity to smell and taste can affect their eating habits. Over-sensitivity to touch can affect their tolerance to the physical proximity of other people.

- *Echolalia*

  Children with autism have significant difficulties in developing language, and some may never develop functional language skills. However, a characteristic of those who do develop speech is to repeat whole sentences or phrases that they have heard, often with the exact intonation and emphasis of the original speaker.

Children with autism are usually educated in schools for children who have severe learning difficulties because they require particular approaches to support learning and to reduce their anxiety. Routine, care and structure are important for this group of pupils. Inability to communicate often leads to frustration and results in behaviour difficulties. If you support a child with autism you will need to work closely with the teacher to implement specific programmes designed to aid communication, e.g. Picture Exchange Communication System (PECS).

Asperger's Syndrome

Asperger's Syndrome (AS) was first identified by Hans Asperger in 1944 and is now used to describe more able children with autistic characteristics. However, there is still some debate about whether Asperger's Syndrome and autism are distinct, but similar conditions, or part of the same overall condition. A number of terms are used by various professionals to indicate that a child's difficulties fall into the same general area. The term 'Autistic Continuum' has been used widely to illustrate that a child's autistic characteristics can range from very severe, to relatively mild. More recently, Lorna Wing introduced the term 'Autistic Spectrum', to represent the complexities involved in assessing the degree of difficulty in different areas of need. The idea of a spectrum better illustrates the fact that each individual child's needs can range in severity across a number of different skills.

The Triad of Impairments

Since the original identification of autistic spectrum disorders, there has been much research that has sought to identify a clearer pattern to the difficulties first identified by Kanner and Asperger. Lorna Wing recognised that although the pattern of difficulties identified seemed quite diverse, many of the characteristics could be grouped together in broad areas of skill. She categorised the key features of Asperger's Syndrome and autism into three main areas of difficulties, which she called the 'Triad of Impairments' (see Figure 10.1).

Although children with Asperger's Syndrome or autism may show additional impairments not covered in the triad, these are not considered essential for diagnosis. What distinguishes autism and Asperger's Syndrome is the nature and degree of difficulty within the different parts of the triad.

For educational purposes, the distinction between the two labels has little impact upon the choice of effective intervention as what we seek to do in schools is to take into account each child's individual difficulties, including the different language needs of each child. An

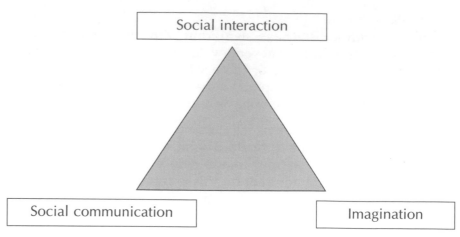

Figure 10.1 The Triad of Impairments

educational approach should also focus on current needs rather than past difficulties.

Asperger's Syndrome is thought to be a form of autism, and children with Asperger's Syndrome share many of the characteristics of autism, but in a milder, or different form. This does not mean to say that the impact of Asperger's Syndrome on a child's ability to function is not significant, and it can be particularly hard for the child because a lot of the time the child appears to behave normally.

Individual differences in age, general ability, personality, home background and general experience will all affect a child's behaviour, and thus the nature of their individual needs. Some children manage to 'hold things together ' at school, but the impact of the difficulties they experience may be felt at home, showing themselves in extreme anxiety, or challenging behaviour. In contrast, some children have more difficulties at school than at home because they are being expected to cope in a more demanding social situation, which provides them with little or no control over what happens to them.

What are the features of Asperger's Syndrome?

Not every child will show all of the difficulties described, or to the degree given in the examples. They may show difficulties in some but not all different situations, or may show more features when under stress.

Social interaction

Impairments in social interaction may include:

- Difficulties in interacting with others, especially other children, who can find them odd and awkward in their attempts at making friendships.

    There is probably less difficulty with adults, because adults are better able to adapt their own behaviour and responses to make the interaction easier, and are probably more tolerant of odd behaviour.

- An inability to apply to the unwritten rules of social interaction. They may not be able to adapt their behaviour to a particular context, e.g. knowing that it's all right to talk loudly in the park, but not in the middle of a church service. Or that it's acceptable to strip down to their underwear in the garden at home if it's hot, but not in the middle of the supermarket.
- A difficulty in adapting their behaviour towards different people. Some children with AS may be over-affectionate towards everyone they meet, not realising that what is an acceptable response to your mother, is not acceptable for your teacher, or a stranger. This is significant in terms of personal safety issues.
- A specific difficulty in recognising emotion in themselves, and in others. Thus they have difficulty in empathising with how others feel, and so cannot provide social support to others in the same way that most of us do. They may learn some of the behaviours expected of them in certain situations (e.g. putting their arm around someone who is crying), but do not actually understand the deeper meaning behind the crying, or their own learned response.
- Less of an interest than most children in pleasing others and seeking approval. This can cause difficulties in trying to motivate a child, as they may not respond to praise, but will require more concrete rewards.
- Because of differences in their understanding of emotion, there may be a difficulty in recognising the importance of facial expression, body language and voice intonation, and the messages that these convey about how another person is feeling.
- A lack of empathy means that individual's with AS do not recognise that what they say and do may upset or embarrass others.

They tend to say exactly what they mean without any thought of consequences and do not recognise the need to keep certain thoughts to themselves, or to adapt what they say to avoid hurting someone's feelings. Thus they may quite happily state a point of fact – that someone is fat, or that their singing is out of tune.

Social communication

Although basic language skills appear to be at least average, closer investigation of how the child with AS uses language, and of their actual understanding of what is being said, reveals significant difficulties with the functional use of language. Verbal language itself represents only a small part of what is needed for effective communication, and children with AS can have a range of difficulties in recognising and using the wider methods of communication:

- Literal interpretation of language, so that the child follows what is being said word for word, and no more. This can lead to misunderstanding of instructions and comments which could be interpreted in different ways, or when metaphors or colloquial phrases are used, e.g.:
    Stand on one foot.
    Pull your socks up.
    Over the moon.

Under the weather.

Take it easy.

Pulling your leg.

Some phrases may, understandably provoke distress:

Laugh your head off.

Killing time.

Butterflies in your stomach.

Further difficulties may be caused in a school setting by instructions which are incomplete, but which assume that the child knows the underlying intention:

Off you go (meaning go back to your tables and start working).

It's getting noisy in here (meaning work more quietly).

Certain instructions may elicit a response from the child that makes it seem that they are being deliberately cheeky:

Can you turn the page over? ('Yes').

Do you know what this shape is called? ('Yes').

- When faced with ambiguous or confusing verbal messages, unlike other children, the child with AS does not have the skills to use other cues to interpret the real meaning behind what is being said. So, if they are told 'That's OK' or 'I'm all right', by someone whose body language is actually saying the opposite, they will understand only the words, and may, as a result come across as unfeeling. These difficulties are exacerbated by the fact that we rarely actually say what we mean. For example, when we meet someone we know, and greet them with 'How are you?' we don't really want a list of their current woes, but are just being polite.

- Individuals with AS have particular difficulties initiating, sustaining and repairing conversation. They may happily talk for hours about a topic that interests them, but will not take the other persons prior knowledge, or interests into account, and may abruptly end the conversation once they have run out of things to say. They find it difficult to apply the subtle rules of listening, reflecting and turn-taking that characterise normal conversation.

- Eye contact is a common problem. In normal communication, we use eye contact to punctuate an interaction, to signify our level of interest, and to confirm joint understanding. Often, individual's with AS avoid eye contact altogether, or use it inappropriately, increasing the awkwardness of communication.

Imagination

Difficulties in imagination encompass a range of behaviours that indicate a basic lack of flexibility in the thinking of children with AS, and a tendency to have a limited repertoire of interests and responses. Difficulties in this area may include:

- Symbolic and imaginative play is later to develop, and the extent to which the child engages in imaginative games or activities at an even later age is often limited. There tends to be a preference for factual information over fictional materials. Fictional preferences are for explicit horror stories (which over emphasise emotions), or science fiction.

- A genuine difficulty in coping with change, sometimes to the extent that they will become extremely distressed when there is an unexpected change in normal routine. This has implications for their reactions when their class is covered by a different teacher, when the times or venues of lessons have to be changed unexpectedly, or when the general school routine is disrupted (e.g. at Christmas time). For some children, even small changes in the layout of a room can cause extreme distress.
- A tendency to become absorbed in particular interests, to the exclusion of other activities. In some cases this can interfere with the child's learning, or with that of others in the class. Interests are often unusual, and commonly involve collecting objects or facts.
- The development of elaborate rituals that do not serve any obvious purpose, other than allowing the child a degree of active control over their surroundings (e.g. having to walk a particular route to school, perhaps touching certain objects on the way; setting out equipment in a specific order before beginning a task).
- A difficulty in generalising skills and adapting what they have learned to different circumstances e.g. the child who has learned the reception class routine of going to the toilet, washing their hands, and putting their coat on before lining up to go out to play, becomes stuck in that routine – putting their coat on and waiting by the door, each time they go to the toilet, regardless of the time of day.

  The older child who learns a mathematical operation in a maths lesson, but needs to be separately taught the same skill in geography and science in order to apply it in a different context.

How is Asperger's Syndrome diagnosed?

Asperger's Syndrome is normally a medical diagnosis. There is no blood test or brain scan which can do this. It is done by identifying the characteristic behaviours. Some professionals are reluctant to make a diagnosis because of fears about the negative effects of labelling children. However, a diagnosis can confirm in some people's eyes that a child's problems have a genuine root.

It is important for children with Asperger's Syndrome that educational planning takes into account the very specific differences in the way that their skills have developed (or failed to develop). The label of Asperger's Syndrome should been seen as a signpost, or starting point, not a sentence or excuse for inaction.

How can I support a child with Asperger's Syndrome?

Before you start, you need to remember the responsibility for meeting the needs of a child with Asperger's Syndrome should not rest with one person. As an assistant you will need to liaise closely with the teacher or SENCO who remains responsible for overall planning and educational development, and any other learning support staff working with the child.

It is crucial that all staff working in a school have at least a basic level of understanding of the underlying factors that affect the behaviour and learning of a child with Asperger's Syndrome.

So, how can I give effective support?

As an assistant you will probably need to give support in each of the different areas of need. This section has practical ideas to help you do this in the area of behaviour.

Developing social skills

In Asperger's Syndrome the fundamental difficulty is in coping with the social world, and responding to the behaviour of others. The idea that people with Autistic Spectrum Disorders should be seen as having their own unique *culture* enables us to think carefully about how we target the needs of individuals with Asperger's Syndrome. It is not our job to force normality upon them. To try and do so overlooks the fact that the underlying patterns of thinking are not inferior, but different. What causes difficulty is our expectations.

Different cultures have their own unique expectations for behaviour. Within a school situation, many of the situations that we place children in are themselves artificial. Educational intervention needs to focus on teaching those with Asperger's Syndrome new skills in order to help them to cope with our culture, and our social world.

Play skills

Observation of early play skills in children with Asperger's Syndrome indicates that they differ from those of normally developing children.

There is a greater tendency to impose order, sorting and lining up toys, rather than playing with them imaginatively. The development of pretend play occurs later or not at all, and there is often a lack of role play and social play.

It has been suggested that social skills development in children with Autistic Spectrum Disorders can be improved through direct adult intervention aimed at developing more normal play skills. Intervention could include:

- Playing alongside the child, gently encouraging them to use toys more flexibly and modelling how to use objects in different ways.
- Encourage dressing up and role play, through active adult participation.
- Active teaching of play skills following close observation of how the peer group play together, what language they use and which games they prefer. The adult can then act the role of another child in a play situation, teaching the child with AS what to say and what to do. Introduce other children into the games gradually, being careful in your selection of playmates.

Developing emotional understanding

Social skills require empathy and an understanding of how another person is feeling and what they are thinking. In many cases a child with Asperger's Syndrome may have learned appropriate responses, i.e. what to do if someone has fallen over, or is angry, but will have no real understanding of the emotions involved. Their actions are mechanical, not empathetic. It can be surprising how poorly some children with Asperger's Syndrome are able to grasp their own emotions.

Developing the child's understanding of their own emotions

For many children, intervention will need to start at the basics. One way suggested by Tony Attwood (1998) is to help the child to create a collection of things which produce a happy emotion, and link them to outward signs of happiness/pleasure by creating a 'Happy Book', which is essentially a scrapbook (or even a box) containing:

- Pictures/objects/photos of things that the child likes.
- Photos and pictures of smiling faces.
- Lists or pictures of things that the child likes to do.
- Favourite colours, animals, music, textures, noises, etc.
- A happy thermometer, or similar, scale, that enables the child to indicate degrees of happiness – how happy they are feeling, or how happy something makes them.
- Pictures of things that make people close to them happy (e.g. mother, father, teacher, friend).

The 'Happy Book' can be used as an ongoing resource to help the child indicate their own level of feeling. It can also be used to help to cheer them up when they are feeling angry or sad. This could be extended to look at contrasting emotions, e.g. sad/happy; angry/calm.

Developing an understanding what affects emotions

The book *Teaching Children with Autism to Mind Read* (Hadwin and Baron-Cohen) is an excellent resource for assessing a child's level of emotional development, and for providing practical activities to develop that understanding. The exercises in the accompanying workbook take the child through the stages of normal development of emotional understanding. This book can be used as a guide for developing emotional understanding for younger children with Asperger's Syndrome. Teaching should be supported by practical activities which draw the child's attention to their own emotions and which focus on the child's own experiences and preferences. Opportunities should then be taken to bring to the child's attention the behaviour of other children that indicates a particular emotion.

Disclosure of emotions

Children with Asperger's Syndrome of all ages find it difficult to identify and share their emotions. This can cause particular difficulties in adolescence where the young person may feel increasingly isolated and not be able to communicate how they are feeling. It is a fact that young people with Asperger's Syndrome are particularly prone to mental health problems and it is not always easy for others to recognise the danger signals.

It is often easier for a child with Asperger's Syndrome to indicate their emotions through visual means. Regular opportunities should be taken to encourage all children with AS to share their level of emotion through pointing at happiness thermometers (or similar visual representations). Older children should also be encouraged to disclose their feelings, and can be given a wider range of faces showing a more complex variety of emotions to select.

Personal safety

Difficulties in understanding the thoughts and intentions of others can lead to particular problems in understanding the potential danger presented by strangers, or by people not very well known to the child or family. Children with Asperger's Syndrome are particularly vulnerable because their own lack of inhibition often leads to over familiarity in terms of affection, touch and proximity.

It is important that children who are likely to be vulnerable are taught specific rules about what is appropriate language to use, and levels of affection to show to different people. This can be done by getting the child to categorise people into a set of circles of friends, and then setting rules for the child about how to act towards people in the different circles:

Centre Circle:	Close family
Second Circle:	Special friends
Third Circle:	General friends
Fourth Circle:	Acquaintances
Fifth Circle:	Strangers

This could also be illustrated to the child through a traffic light system, e.g:

RED:	Don't speak to *strangers*
AMBER:	Smiles and chats are OK for *friends and acquaintances*
GREEN:	Hugs and kisses are OK for *family*

Teaching social skills

Unlike most of us individuals with Asperger's Syndrome do not acquire an intuitive grasp of social skills as part of their normal development. Instead, specific teaching is needed to explain social situations and to train the child how to interact with others. Many individuals with Asperger's' Syndrome do eventually develop a degree of social skill, but very much at a learned, rather than intuitive level.

Standard social skills groups will not always cater for the particular needs of a child with Asperger's Syndrome.

Any teaching should focus upon individual needs and the pattern of difficulties for each child will be different. Careful observation of how the child interacts with others will highlight the particular difficulties that they face, and so the priority needs for teaching. Often we are simply teaching specific strategies for coping in a school situation.

The adult with Asperger's Syndrome at least has some choice about which social situations they put themselves in, and so some of the difficulties that may cause a child or others significant problems at school do not arise in adulthood.

You need to remember these important factors

- Do not force a child into social situations in the hope that through mixing with others they will pick up social skills.
- Teach specific skills, as far as possible in the context in which they will be used.
- Provide opportunities for the child to practise their skills in safe situations, e.g. with adults, and sympathetic children.
- Teach the child specifically about friendships (What makes a good friend? What does a good friend do? etc.).
- Provide positive reinforcements and rewards to encourage the use of appropriate social skills.

Support from other children

Social skills, by their very nature, involve interaction with others. Most children quickly recognise that there is something different about the child with Asperger's Syndrome, and intuitively treat them differently. Many children do their best to help, but can be rebuffed, affecting their own self-esteem.

Other children will learn to avoid the child with Asperger's Syndrome because they simply do not know how to treat them. Unfortunately, it is also in the nature of some children to exploit an individual with Asperger's Syndrome because of their very naïvety.

There is sometimes a reluctance to involve others in support because of a fear that by doing so we will draw attention to the child with Asperger's Syndrome as being different, and somehow break a confidence.

However, the child's peer group already know that they are different and will be better able to understand and support them if they are actively involved in thinking of ways to help.

As an assistant your role is really important in encouraging other children to include the child with Asperger's Syndrome and accept their differences as part of the class group.

Supporting behaviour

The majority of behaviour problems arise out of anxiety, or not understanding hidden rules of behaviour. Proactive strategies will help to alleviate much of the anxiety, and so reduce problem behaviour. Basic guidelines for addressing behaviour include reducing anxiety and stress through:

- Adapting the physical environment.
- Providing secure and consistent routines.
- Placing appropriate demands upon the child.
- Planning ahead for strategies that reduce the likelihood of behaviour problems.
- Knowing the child's anxiety triggers.
- Knowing the signs of increasing stress.
- Anticipating potential areas of difficulty.

Try to anticipate tricky situations

Responding sensitively to problem behaviour:

- Be aware of the effect of AS on behaviour.
- Be consistent.
- Stay in control.
- Teach new skills that the problem behaviour indicates is needed.

Some problem behaviour can arise because specific factors in the environment or situation are causing anxiety and triggering an inappropriate response. It is important to try and identify those triggers so that you can adapt the environment and your own expectations and behaviour:

- Ask the child.
- Look at the task.
- Attention during instruction.
- Response to instruction.
- Language issues.
- Ability to complete task.
- Time on task.
- Internal distractions.
- Look at the classroom environment.
- Potential stress factors.
- Potential distractions.
- Influence of other members of the class.

Obsessions

- Recognise that obsessions serve a purpose for the child with Asperger's Syndrome.

- Provide regular opportunities for engaging in obsessive behaviour, but maintain control by setting aside specific times that reduce the interference on the child's learning or that of others.
- Ignore minor obsessive behaviours unless they present a problem.
- Don't attempt to eliminate an obsession unless there are significant reasons for doing so. A less controllable obsession may take its place!
- Build academic activities around obsessions.
- Use obsessions as a reward.
- Monitor the level of obsessive behaviour as an indication of increasing stress.

Maintaining control

Individuals with Asperger's Syndrome can be very stubborn because of their inflexible view of the world, and often egocentric expectations.

It will sometimes be necessary to allow the child to apparently get their own way because confrontation will only escalate a difficult situation. In such instances it is important to follow up incidents with the child as soon as possible, and take action to reduce the risk of similar incidents occurring. This could be achieved through using *The New Social Story Book* approach, or *Comic Strip Conversations* to show the child that the behaviour was not appropriate, and to teach new rules or alternative behaviour.

Where an individual with Asperger's Syndrome attempts to impose their will and refuses to carry out certain tasks, a strict behaviour management system should be introduced to ensure that the adult maintains control. Initially it may be necessary to use a low demand-high reward system, so that the child receives a high value reward for what may seem to be minimal compliance. Gradually, the task expectations should be increased and the reward level reduced. In all cases it is crucial that the reward is truly rewarding for the particular child. Obsessions come in useful here!

Sanctions can be applied as for any other child. However, it is important that you have first made sure that you have not overlooked an aspect of Asperger's Syndrome that may be:

- Preventing the child from achieving their target.
- Causing anxiety.

Motivation

When working with children with Asperger's Syndrome it is sometimes hard to find rewards that motivate as these children are less responsive to praise and attention than most. They cannot see the immediate purpose for a task, they may dismiss it as irrelevant. They are more likely to respond to tangible rewards or tokens so do bear this in mind when trying to motivate the child you are working with.

To provide external motivation, try to ensure that:

- The subject interests the child.
- The child can see a real purpose to the task.
- The purpose of the task is explained clearly in terms of learning gains.

- The child has the incentive of a concrete reward for completing the task.

Changing the physical environment

The busy, often cramped environment of the classroom can produce particular behaviour problems for the child with Asperger's Syndrome.

The need for personal space and particular difficulties with physical proximity can cause anxiety and lead to aggressive behaviour towards others. Visual distractions can affect the child's attention and concentration. Difficulties can be prevented by:

- Providing an individual work area to be used for all or part of the time.
- Placing the child on a group table in a less distracting area of the classroom.
- Screening-off potential distractions.
- Being aware of potential stress triggers (e.g. noise/glare).
- Clear labelling of classroom areas.
- Allowing the child to leave or enter the room before or after others, to avoid the crush.
- Allowing the child to use a favourite chair/table.

Providing structure

Much anxiety which can lead to behaviour difficulties is caused through the child's inability to cope with waiting, as well as coping with apparently open-ended tasks. The child's concept of time is often not well developed, and this can add to the uncertainty, increasing anxiety levels. You can:

- Ensure consistency in your approach.
- Wherever possible work to a consistent timetable.
- Provide the child with a visual timetable or work schedule.
- Give the child as much information as possible about what is going to happen (preferably written).
- Give the child warning when an activity is due to change.
- Prepare the child well in advance for any change in routine.

KEY POINT

Listen to the child. Observe the child. Try to see things from the child's perspective.

Chapter 11

Some 'What ifs...? and what to do

Be assured that, for most of the time, things will run smoothly and your common sense will guide your responses. However, from time to time there may be incidents which leave you unsure about how to respond.

Here are some 'worst fear' scenarios which assistants have shared. They may help you to do the right thing when things go wrong! (the answers are on page 97.)

1. What if...?
   You are working in a separate room from the teacher and a child in your group runs out of the room in an angry or upset mood.
   Should you:
   a) Run after him leaving the rest of the group behind?
   b) Let the teacher know immediately?
   c) Pretend it hasn't happened and hope he comes back?

2. What if...?
   You are working with a group and a child starts a fight with another.
   Should you:
   a) Say 'Stop fighting and sit down' in a firm assertive voice?
   b) Immediately try to separate the pair?
   c) Ignore the action and praise the others in the group for getting on with their work?

3. What if...?
   You ask a pupil to do something and they respond by swearing at you.
   Should you:
   a) Be rude back?
   b) Ignore it and hope it won't happen again?
   c) Ask 'Is that a respectful thing to do?' and point out that a school rule is 'no swearing'. Give them a warning and say that if it happens again you will report the behaviour to the teacher.

4. What if...?
   You notice bruises on the pupil's body.
   Should you:
   a) Question them about it?
   b) Call Social Services?
   c) Report it to the teacher?

5. What if...?

   You find some pupils smoking round the back of the school buildings.

   Should you:

   a) Ask them to come back to the playground?

   b) Report the incident to the head of year?

   c) Ignore it?

6. What if...?

   The teacher is getting stressed and has a go unfairly at the pupil you work with.

   Should you:

   a) Protest?

   b) Speak to the teacher later?

   c) Speak to the child about the teacher's unfair behaviour?

7. What if...?

   You meet the parent of a pupil you work with in the supermarket.

   Should you:

   a) Tell them their child's latest problems?

   b) Ignore them?

   c) Be pleasant and try to say something good about the child?

8. What if...?

   You notice some bullying behaviour from some pupils on the way to school.

   Should you:

   a) Mention it to the teacher when you get to school?

   b) Ignore it?

   c) Stop your car and have a word with the pupils?

9. What if...?

   You have been asked to work with a pupil on a particular task and he or she refuses point blank to do it.

   Should you:

   a) Report it to the teacher?

   b) Ignore the refusal and get on with something else?

   c) Reflect the pupil's feelings and offer to help them with it?

10. What if...?

    You are working with a group and one child grabs a screwdriver and starts threatening another child.

    Should you:

    a) Grab the screwdriver from the child's hand?

    b) Say in a firm voice 'Michael, put the screwdriver down *now*'?

    c) Call the teacher?

11. What if...?

    You are accused (wrongly) by a pupil of hitting him or her and the pupil has complained to the teacher and to his or her parents.

    Should you:

    a) Talk to the teacher about the alleged incident?

    b) Write a report about your experience of the time when the alleged incident took place?

    c) Go round to the pupil's home to discuss what really happened with the parents?

12. What if...?
    You are working with a group and a purse, belonging to a pupil, goes missing.
    Should you:
    a) Keep all the pupils in at playtime until someone owns up?
    b) Report it to the teacher?
    c) Carry out a search of the school bags of those in the group?

13. What if...?
    You are working with a group and you notice a pupil is cutting herself with a sharp object.
    Should you:
    a) Have a quiet word with her then speak to her at the end of the lesson?
    b) Take the object away?
    c) Report the incident to the teacher?

14. What if...?
    You feel uncomfortable because the teacher you work with often uses you as 'the bad guy' (e.g. 'Mark, that's the third time I've told you to stop talking. Go and sit with Mrs Smith' or 'Right, I've had enough, Mrs Smith, will you take him out").
    Should you:
    a) Speak to the teacher about your feelings?
    b) Put up with it?
    c) Protest loudly in the staffroom?

Answers

1. *The answer could be b) or c)* depending on the age of the child and your knowledge of the child's behaviour.
   When children run out of the classroom they are usually feeling stressed and many want or need attention. If you chase after them it will only serve to give the attention and make it likely to happen again so with older children it is probably best not to follow immediately but to send a note via another pupil to the teacher explaining what has happened and to try to find the pupil at the end of the lesson when you can give some support and find out what is wrong. You might ask a friend of the pupil to follow and check that he or she is OK.

   However it is difficult with younger children as there are the safety aspects to consider and you don't want them running out of school. You need a plan to get help quickly. You do need to alert the teacher so that either you or the teacher can follow. If the site is secure it is probably better not to follow and the child will most likely come back under their own steam. If this behaviour keeps happening it is helpful to involve the parent so that they know the risks. Don't leave the group on their own without supervision.

2. *Answer a)*
   A swift and firm instruction is often the best response to an incident of fighting. If this does stop the action, then you need to separate the pair and allow time for 'cooling off'. If you can praise the others in the group for working that may help. You should NOT try to separate the pair unless you can do so safely, you

know the restraint procedure and have the permission of the head teacher to use it. You should call for help or get a pupil to go for a teacher if it is a severe incident.

3. *Answer c)*

    Your emotional reaction might be to be rude back but this will not help things and will up the stakes. You could try ignoring it at the time then take it up with the pupil at the end of the lesson pointing out that it is not a respectful way to behave.

    You should certainly show some response and to point out that it is not acceptable. In saying you will speak to the teacher if it happens again, you are giving an appropriate warning.

4. *Answer c)*

    If you spot what you consider are signs of abuse, you should always report it to the teacher rather than asking the child about it or taking matters into your own hands. You should certainly not ignore it. If bruises are on the arms or legs you could ask 'Have you fallen over?' but beware of asking leading questions. Questioning is best managed by the teacher.

5. *Answer a) and b)*

    If you catch pupils smoking your should ask them to put their cigarettes out and return to the playground. You should also report the incident to the head of year and try to identify who the pupils are. If you ignore it, it is likely to happen again and helps to create an ethos of 'It's not my problem' which is not helpful in maintaining status and respect.

6. *Answer b)*

    Your gut reaction may be to speak up in the pupil's defence especially if it is unfair. It depends on your relationship with the teacher, you might, rather than a protest, point out some facts, 'Mr Brown, I don't think you saw that Kerry was poking Julie before she screamed'. It may be better in some cases to wait until the end of the lesson when you can have a word about what really happened. If the teacher does not accept your point you should share it with the teacher who manages your work. It is important that pupils see adults as working together in order that:

    *   They do not feel they can play one off against the other.
    *   Teachers who are stressed feel supported, not undermined. Sometimes you might want to make a 'smoothing' comment to the pupil, but try not to undermine the teacher.

7. *Answer c)*

    It is really important to maintain confidentiality about what goes on at school and it is NOT your role to share any bad news about the child. It will help things if you can keep to pleasant social chat possibly saying something positive about the child.

8. *Answer a) and possibly c)*

    If you notice bullying you should certainly mention it to the teacher when you get to school as it may affect the way the children come into school and continue into lesson time. If a child is being attacked you may well want to stop and say something 'Get yourselves to school now and stop that behaviour.' If it persists you may need to warn the group that you will be reporting the incident.

The school staff are only responsible for what goes on, on school premises, but parents may need to be informed if the incident is severe.

9. *Answer c) and possibly b)*
    Reflecting the pupil's feelings about the task is often the first step in getting them to 'thaw' a little. Giving a reason why they should do it is also a good move, as is putting it back to the pupil as a choice. Then offering support to get started will be helpful especially if the pupil views the task as too hard, e.g. 'I know you don't want to do this but if you choose not to do it you'll be in trouble and neither you nor I want that. Come on let's look at what's needed and I'll see how I can help.'

    The strategy of ignoring might be a good one if you think the pupil is refusing to gain attention rather than just stubborness. If you do ignore sometimes the pupil will start to do the task. If this fails then response c) can be used. If both b) and c) have not worked you will need to report what has happened to the teacher.

10. *Answer b) and c)*
    This incident cannot be ignored, someone may get hurt. Saying the child's name in a firm clear voice will alert them and hopefully stop them from waving the screwdriver about.

    Giving a clear instruction 'Put the screwdriver down now' is also a good strategy as it is a simple command which is likely to be obeyed if you give it in an assertive voice. With young children you may feel you are able to move from behind the child and physically remove the screwdriver, but do be careful and hold the child's lower arm rather than grabbing the screwdriver directly.

11. *Answer a) and b)*
    This is a very upsetting thing to happen and you will feel hurt, angry and upset. Your first reaction might be to call the pupil a liar but it is best to stay calm and say to the pupil 'Gemma, you know that's not true.' It is really important that you don't take matters into your own hands, go round to the pupil's house or confront the pupil by yourself. You should certainly talk to the class teacher about the alleged incident and write down your version of events as soon as you are able to on the same day if possible. A third party will be able to handle the incident professionally and sensitively. You will find you will get support from school staff and often from the parents once the allegation has been investigated. In the rare case of the parents continuing to back the child's accusations the head may need to refer the incident on.

12. *Answer b)*
    This is a tricky situation and one which you should report to the teacher before the group have dispersed so that he or she can speak to the group and sort it out. It is not a legal strategy to punish the whole group by keeping them in because it is not fair to the majority and only breeds resentment. The teacher may want to question members of the group one by one and invite information from them.

13. *Answer a) and c)*
    You will probably be quite concerned about this behaviour, and rightly so as self-harm can be a feature of depression. A quiet word

will often be enough to stop it happening although you may want to talk to the pupil a little more in a one-to-one situation.

In any case it needs to be reported to the teacher who may want to speak to the pupil's parents about the incident. If you can remove the sharp object without a fuss, then do so.

14. *Answer a)*

It is sometimes the case that assistants are taken advantage of in this way and it is not fair or acceptable. It may be appropriate from time to time for teachers to ask assistants to support them by being with a pupil who has been excluded from the class. This should only happen if the teacher makes it clear to the assistant what they are expected to do with the excluded pupil and where they might do it. Being left 'in limbo' with an angry or unhappy pupil is not an easy situation to manage. It will help to discuss your concerns with the teacher(s) involved or if this is not a realistic option, with the SENCO or the teacher who normally manages your work. You may find it necessary to refer to your job description as this is almost certainly beyond the normal expectations of your role.

KEY POINT

Question your approach. If it works, do more of it. If it doesn't work, do something different.

Answers to questions on page 36:

1, 3, 5, 7 are clear

2, 4, 6, 8 are fuzzy

Key points to remember in helping children to manage their behaviour

1. Behaviours are learned and can be changed.
2. Overnight changes are unlikely. It has taken a long time for the child to get to their present point and it may take some time for positive changes to be seen – so don't give up.
3. Children seek to 'belong' to the group. Sometimes they don't know how to behave in order to do this effectively. You can help them learn new skills so they can achieve this.
4. The child will not wake up one morning thinking 'I'm going to behave well today.' *You*, as the adult, must be the first one to make the move and change the way you work with the child.
5. Every child needs to be valued. You need to work to develop positive relationships with those children who find it hard to behave or settle to learning.
6. Behaviour is a response to context, environment, other people or the activity. The child is reacting to these factors. It may be that something in the context needs to change, rather than in the child.
7. Listen to the child. Observe the child. Try to see things from the child's perspective.
8. Give the child positive messages – both verbal and non-verbal – every day.
9. When providing a sanction it is consistency not severity which makes it effective.
10. Start each day as a new day. Have positive expectations that the child will improve.
11. *You* are a powerful influence on the child and can be a real force for positive change in the child's behaviour and attitude – don't give up.
12. Question your approach. If it works, do more of it. If it doesn't work, do something different!

Some final comments

The role of the assistant in supporting children and young people whose behaviour is difficult to manage can be very challenging. It certainly requires persistence, dedication, sensitivity and a sense of humour. Positive expectations that behaviour can change are also needed. Some days it may seem an impossible job and this leads to feelings of demoralisation, helplessness or being let down. This is demanding work which often tests human resources to the limit and assistants need frequent support from teachers and effective partnership planning to enable them to be successful in fulfilling this role. There is much evidence to show that the work of assistants helps enormously in enabling many children and young people to stay 'on track' and included in both the social and academic aspects of our schools. Many pupils, when they are older, remember with gratitude the support given by assistants. So it can be an extremely rewarding role which can bring a good deal of job satisfaction.

In this book, I have brought together a range of ideas and strategies which can be used to support children with a range of emotional and behavioural needs. I hope it proves useful in guiding understanding and providing a framework for knowing where to start, what to do and how to do it. I hope too that it enables assistants and teacher/assistant partnerships in supporting this particularly vulnerable group of pupils in our schools.

Physical restraint

What is physical restraint?

Physical restraint is when a member of staff uses force with the intention of restricting a pupil's movements against their will. It should only be used if calming and defusing strategies have failed.

Physical restraint must:

- Involve the minimum force necessary.
- Be applied only until the pupil is calm.
- Be used to de-escalate a potentially dangerous situation.
- Not be used as a threat or punishment.
- Not inflict pain.
- Be administered calmly and rationally, not in response to anger or frustration.
- Be the result of a professional judgement about the pupil's safety, taking into account the age and abilities of the pupil.
- Be in the best interests of the pupil.

When might physical restraint be used?

- When there is a risk of injury to people.
- When there is a risk of significant damage to property.
- Where there is a risk of a criminal offence being committed.
- When a pupil has been restrained it should always be recorded and reported to the head teacher as soon as possible.

But do remember:

- Physical restraint should always be used as a last resort.
- As an adult in the school, working under the guidance of the teacher, you have a duty of care to maintain good order and safeguard the health and safety of pupils.
- You must not run the risk of personal injury by intervening when it is not safe to do so.

References

Attwood, T. (1998) *Asperger's Syndrome: A guide for parents and professionals*. London: Jessica Kingsley Publishers.

Balshaw, M. (1999) 'The management, role and training of learning support assistants'. A research report for the DfEE. University of Manchester, Centre for Educational Needs.

Bernard, M. E. (1995) *You Can Do It! What every student (and parent) should know about school and life*.

Besag, V. (1989) *Bullies and Victims in Schools*. Buckingham: Open University Press.

Blatz, W. (1938) *The Five Sisters*.

Bowlby, J. (1953) *Child Care and the Growth of Love*. Harmondsworth: Pelican.

British Household Panel Study (2000) Institute for Social and Economic Research, University of Essex. www.iser.essex.ac.uk

Canter, L. and Canter, M. (1976) *Assertive Discipline: Positive behaviour management for today's classroom*. USA: Lee Canter and Associates.

Children Act (1989) London: HMSO.

Department of Education and Science (DES) (1981) *Education Act*. London: HMSO.

Department of Education and Science (1989) *Discipline in Schools*, Report of the Committee of Enquiry chaired by Lord Elton (The Elton Report). London: HMSO.

DfEE (1998) *Report by the School Exclusion Unit*. London: HMSO.

Dreikurs, R. and Cassel, P. (1972) *Discipline Without Tears*. New York, USA: Plume.

Faupel, A. *et al.* (1998) *Anger Management: A practical guide*. London: David Fulton Publishers.

Gray, C. *Comic Strip Conversations*. Future Horizons Inc; available from Winslow Press.

Gray, C. *The New Social Story Book*. Future Horizons Inc; available from Winslow Press.

Hadwin and Baron-Cohen, S. *Teaching Children with Autism to Mind Read*. Chichester: Wiley.

Hampshire County Council (1996) *Attention Deficit (Hyperactivity) Disorder: Information and guidelines for schools*.

La Vigna, G. W. (1992) *Positive Approaches to Solving Behaviour Challenges 1992*. Los Angeles, CA: Institute for Applied Behaviour Analysis.

Lawrence, D. (1973) *Improved Reading Through Counselling*.

Lorenz, S. (1998) *Effective In Class Support*. London: David Fulton Publishers.

Maines, B. and Robinson, G. (1988) *You Can ... You Know You Can: A self-concept approach*. Bristol: Lucky Duck Publications.

Maines, B. and Robinson, G. (1988) 'A bag of tricks' Bristol: Lucky Duck Publications.

Maines, B. and Robinson, G. (1993) *The No Blame Approach*. Bristol: Lucky Duck Publications.

Mallon, B. (1987) *An Introduction to Counselling Skills for Special Educational Needs*. Manchester: Manchester University Press.

Maslow, A. (1954) *Motivation and Personality*. New York: Harper and Row.

Mental Health Foundation 'All about ADHD' (Tel: 020 7535 7420)

O'Rourke, K. and Worzbyt, J. C. (1996) *Support Groups for Children: Accelerated development*. USA: Taylor and Francis Group.

Poole Educational Psychology Service (2001) *Anger Management: A six session course*. Poole, Dorset: Educational Psychology Service, Borough of Poole.

Valentine, C. W. (1956) *The Normal Child*. Harmondsworth. Pelican.

Vernon-Allen, S. (2001) *A Guide to Supporting Children with Asperger's Syndrome in School*. Poole, Dorset: Poole LEA.